◆ **HOW TO** ◆

RockClimb!

John Long

◮

CHOCKSTONE PRESS

Evergreen, Colorado
1989

HOW TO ROCK CLIMB!

Cover and book design by Jack Atkinson

Page layout done on a Macintosh SE with Quark Xpress, output on a Linotronic L300.

Cover photograph by Mark Chapman: Ed Barry on "Powerline" (5.12b), Smith Rock, Oregon.

Library of Congress Cataloging in Publication Data

Long, John, 1954-
    How to rock climb! / John Long.
        p.   cm.
    ISBN 0-934641-20-X
    1. Rock climbing.   I. Title.
    GV200.2.L66   1989
    796.5'223–dc20

ISBN 0-934641-20-X

Published and distributed by

Chockstone Press, Inc.
Post Office Box 3505
Evergreen, Colorado 80439

Acknowledgements

No one climber is the living authority on all the technical information and equipment covered in *Rock Climb!* Consequently, the manuscript passed through many expert hands to insure the facts were both up to date and as accurate as possible. In particular, I'd like to thank Bob Gaines, of Vertical Adventures, Charles Cole, of the Five Ten Company, and Russ Walling, of Fish Products, whose suggestions were invaluable. Thanks also to Neptune Mountaineering, The Boulder Mountaineer, Colorado Outdoor Sports, and Chouinard Equipment, who provided equipment for testing and photographing. The clean illustrations and line drawings were handled by Marj Leggitt and Annie Douden. Sharon Sadleir spent many chilly days posing for photos, and always looked hale doing so. After he excerpted text for his magazine, *Climbing Magazine* editor Michael Kennedy further obliged us by writing the foreword, probably the best endorsement we could ever get. Paul Edwards combed over the text, quickly pointing out where things weren't as clear as they should be.

Lastly, this book would only be so many words without the tireless labor of publisher George Meyers, who simply wanted the pre-eminent how-to book and gave me no peace until he felt he had it. George had his guiding hand in virtually every phase of this manual, and if there is any excellence found herein, it's probably due more to George's efforts than my own.

Warning

This is an instruction book to a potentially dangerous activity. It is not intended to be the only source of information for those wishing to pursue the sport of rock climbing. Supplemental instruction by certified rock climbing instructors is necessary to obtain the safest use of this book. By the use of this book, the reader hereby releases the author, publisher, and distributor of How to Rock Climb! from liability for any injury, including death, that might result.

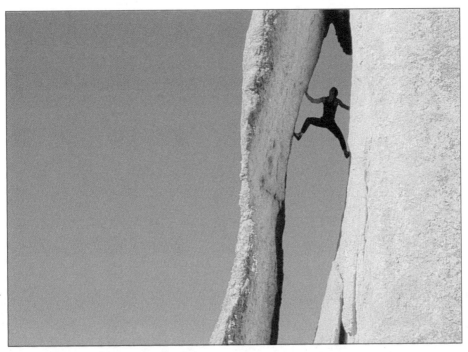

Bob Gaines photo

C O N T E N T S

HOW TO ROCK CLIMB!

JOHN LONG

Foreword

When I started climbing twenty years ago, my friends and I learned our craft by trial and error, mostly from other climbers barely more experienced than we were. We made lots of mistakes, but were afraid enough (and conservative enough) to insure our survival through these critical beginning years. And so we muddled along, gradually working up through the grades as our skills evolved, and having many wonderful epics (at least in retrospect) along the way.

HOW TO ROCK CLIMB!

JOHN LONG

The books we turned to were many: *Annapurna, The White Spider, Nanga Parbat Pilgrimage,* and the other great mountaineering classics inspired, but didn't say much about how our heroes learned the tricks of the trade. And one of the few instructional texts then available, *Mountaineering, Freedom of the Hills,* while offering a great overview of classic mountaincraft, was weak in its treatment of the arena which most inflamed our young hearts: that of technical rock climbing.

Then along came *Basic Rockcraft* and *Advanced Rockcraft.* Written by Royal Robbins, one of the top practioners of the day, these two slim volumes of wit and wisdom served to both inspire and instruct a whole generation of American rock climbers.

Now, nearly twenty years later, much has changed in the sport. New gear, a greater diversity in style, and a rapidly-expanding population of technical rock climbers has dated much of the information in the *Rockcraft* series. Yet there has been precious little to takes its place, at least until now.

John Long is one of that generation of climbers inspired by Robbins' books, and many of today's climbers will find similar inspiration here. Long's broad experience as a pioneering free climber is evident on every page of *Rock Climb!* as, in clear, concise, and entertaining prose, he brings to life the vitality and intricacy of modern technical rock climbing in all its diverse forms.

And while this book may prevent a few epics of the sort I had while learning the ropes, it will help instill a sense of personal responsibility in the reader as well. After all, that's still a big part of what climbing is all about.

MICHAEL KENNEDY
Climbing Magazine

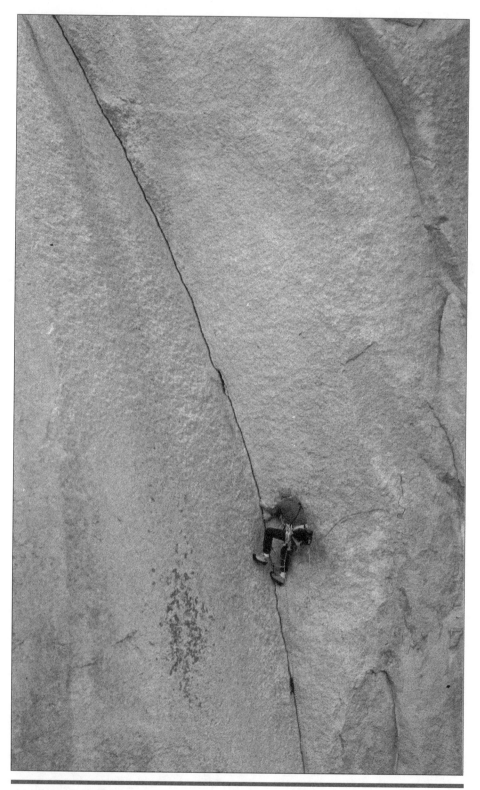

The Sport Climbing Game

Remember that Spencer Tracy movie where the plane crashes on a nether plateau and Spencer flakes out the rope and conducts a glorious rescue? I was about thirteen when I saw that movie and I really wanted to learn all those rope shenanigans, so I jogged to the library and checked out a book on climbing. That manual was fantastic for all its knots and puzzling rope constructs, suspect poetry and narratives of horror and heroics on the cliffside. And I understood none of it. What I needed was a brass tacks, how-to book which assumed I knew nothing, and which broke it all down in plain English.

Since that first outing to the library, rock climbing has boomed. Along with the countless climbing schools, several outstanding instruction books have appeared. However, evolutions in equipment and technique have gone far beyond even the best of these. "Sport climbing"—the attitude of approaching climbing as a serious athletic endeavor—has virtually replaced the quaint notions of Spencer Tracy taking on the mountain. The sport has come of age, and the time is ripe for a modern treatment of climbing from the ground up.

This book is based on the Yosemite system, methods born out of the revolutionary climbs of the fifties and sixties in Yosemite Valley, climbs that changed the face of rock climbing forever. The Yosemite system stresses safety and simplicity, and has become the standardized method throughout America and much of the rock climbing world. Specialized techniques not inherent in the Yosemite system have been incorporated into this book if their utility was thought useful to the sport climber. We have tried to frame the entire process with enough depth that the beginner—and even the advanced climber—can take something from the reading and safely discover how it applies to their own climbing.

•

The average person has never seen a climbing documentary or perused a climbing magazine, so his notions about climbing are limited to the version served up on the big screen—absurd as it is false: The weathered veteran with the Frankenstein boots and the pack resembling a grand piano, marooned on the vertical cliff, the scaly rock peeling away under hand and foot. He's desperate. He slaps, the hand-hold pops and he plummets. The frayed hemp rope

(page opposite)

John Jurachek liebacks up the razorcut dihedral on "Forest Lawn" (5.9), at Cochise's Stronghold, Arizona.

Bill Hatcher photo

parts like taffy and the veteran, arms windmilling, whistles into the void, his scream echoing down the valley. Or perhaps, it's the dauntless Marine, teetering on a slim shelf below impassable stone. He hurls the grappling hook, and though its purchase is something less than a frozen cobweb, he handwalks up the rope like it's tied off to a tug-boat stanchion. Rest assured that both these examples represent sport climbing in no way. No sane person would even feign interest in grappling hooks, let alone buy a book to learn to use it. Modern rock climbing never involves climbing up a hand-line and should never require do-or-die tactics. Both means are possible if a persons chooses, but neither portrays what hundreds of thousands of climbers live to do. Statistically, rock climbing is the safest of all the so-called thrill sports because it employs over a century's worth of refined technique and solid technology to the normal end of *having fun*.

The basic system of technical rock climbing—how a rope and specialized techniques and equipment safeguard a climber—is so simple that anyone can manage the fundamentals in a few week-ends. There is no mystery, and one need not be even a decent climber to have a working knowledge of rope management. The actual art of climbing rock is another affair, but even this tends to be more of a learned skill, requiring less natural ability than other sports. I've been astonished more than once by climbers who couldn't begin to dribble a basketball but were watch-and-weep wizards on the rock. Lastly, climbing is not a reaction sport, so there is no reason a game climber cannot carry on at a top level until old age, as many do.

We can discuss equipment in definitive terms. Equipment is tangible, and it's function, at least in theory, is pretty clearcut. The most important element in safe climbing is not equipment, however, but familiarity with the vertical environment. Any way you shake it, climbing prowess is your principal protection as it precludes the necessity of relying on the gear to save you. Do not expect too much from the gear. The leader who relies on the equipment to safeguard his mistakes is far more likely to make them; and even when the back-up system is perfectly arranged, one can still get hurt. In parachuting, even a jump master carries a reserve chute. As a climber, your main chute is your climbing ability; your back up is the equipment. This said, the number of accidents due to defective gear is remarkably low. It's the climber who is safe or dicey, not the gear.

While equipment and its function within the whole system of sport climbing is fairly straightforward, the art of climbing rock is not. A lot of intangibles—judgement, instinct, and physical awareness to list a few—factor heavily in the process, making explanations pretty slippery affairs. The best we can hope for is to explain clearly and in some detail how things are done in a generic sense, leaving you to learn the how of it all through specific application. We've gone into

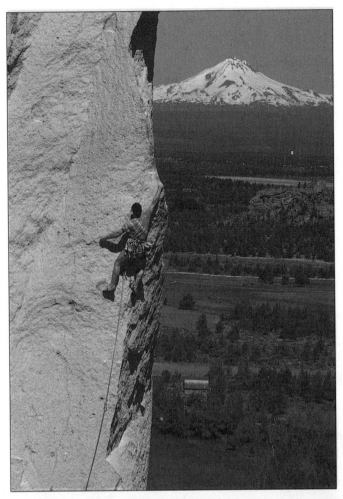

Against an alpine back-drop, Dana Houser clasps the arete on "Spank the Monkey" (5.12a), Smith Rock, Oregon. Many modern testpieces follow steep, outside corners, requiring hearty combinations of face and liebacking techniques.

Greg Epperson photo

exhaustive detail concerning climbing techniques, and in this respect, the book is "back loaded", meaning, a complete novice might find the explanations confusing on the first pass, but the more climbing he does, the more sense and use the book will be.

That climbing transcends mere sport is a conviction held by most anyone with a pair of rock boots, and everyone who has climbed a monolith like Yosemite's El Capitan. Why? The airy exposed routes, the spectacle of ascent, the physical and mental demands—they all give a rush to your blood which continues running rich, regardless of experience. In a flash, mundane life is forgotten: your world is focused down to a scant toehold or saving "jug handle". Failure is a bitter pill, but as Montague noted, nowhere on earth is the taste of success so sweet as on the summit of some sheer granite spire that nearly drove you down in despair from the Herculean labor to achieve it. Basically, it is no more natural for man to dangle on the cliffside than it is for him to loft around the cosmos in the space shuttle; but when both astronauts and climbers gape at their world so very far underfoot, they understand how men have come to dream Gardens of Eden and Ages of Gold. And the dream never fades, the blood never cools, even in the face of chilling bivouacs and knuckle-shredding cracks. Climbing is not easy sport, and it has a lion's share of toil; but to thousands, even millions worldwide, the rewards are worth the struggle.

A NUTSHELL HISTORY OF CLIMBING

Early man was a climber. He climbed to escape predators, to forage for food. Eons later, in the mid-seventeen hundreds, man began climbing again, out of desire, not necessity. Spread throughout the European Alps, villages big and small were nestled between spectacular mountains, and for a host of reasons, certain men aspired to climb the grandest peaks on the continent. The summit was the ultimate goal of these first mountaineers, and glaciers and snow slopes provided the most natural passage to the top. Following the first recorded alpine ascent, that of Mt. Aiguille, the rush was on and major peaks were climbed in succession. After the easier routes had been climbed, subsequent mountaineers found some rock climbing skill was necessary to open up new mountains, and they discovered the lower cliffs and crags provided a perfect training ground to this end. To give some modicum of safety to the falling climber, ropes and rudimentary belaying techniques were introduced around the turn of the twentieth century. While climbing was effectively confined to the European continent, and to a lesser degree in England, it was in Austria—circa 1910—that rappelling was invented, along with heavy steel carabiners (snap links) and pitons, the latter to provide the aid and protection required on the modern, more difficult climbs. With the new equipment and techniques, and the confidence they spawned, Austrian and German climbers established climbs far more difficult than previously thought possible.

Flat-footed in the Flatirons (outside Boulder, Colorado), turn of the century "alpinists" grapple up the hemp rope.

Though isolated rock summits were occasionally bagged, the endeavor was considered of "lesser" worth than achieving the big summits of the Alps. In retrospect, some of the "training climbs" on these "practice" cliffs were remarkably difficult considering the gear. The leaders had little more than hemp ropes (which routinely broke), hemp-soled shoes, and boldness to see them through. Even today, in parts of Eastern Europe, particularly around Dresden, "summitless" crags are eschewed in favor of the spires which abound there; likewise, the method and style of ascent has remained almost unchanged for fifty years.

Meanwhile, in pre-World War I England, rock climbing on the many backyard outcrops was being explored, albeit less aggressively than in Germany. The English discouraged the use of pitons, however, partly for ethical reasons, partly owing to the fragile nature of the "gritstone". Anyway, in the absence of big mountains, the English developed crag climbing as a sport in its own right. In the Americas, the sport's development followed the European lead, though with something of a time delay; roped climbing only arrived in the late 1920s.

The 1930s heralded the golden age of alpine climbing, though the emphasis was still on climbing the major ridges and faces of the higher peaks. During this pre-war period rock climbing standards rose steadily throughout the world, and though most of the glory was still in achieving mountainous summits—Alpine, American, and Asian peaks were conquered in succession—in many areas it was rock climbing standards that saw the most dramatic development.

A thousand feet up and ten feet out on a ring-angle peg, the late, great Willi Unsoeld (first American ascent of Mt. Everest) teeters up the "knobby wall" during the first ascent of El Capitan's East Buttress in 1953. This climb set the standard for the long, classic free climbs which remain the international draw of Yosemite Valley, California.

Allen Steck photo

World War II saw little climbing activity, but the war prompted technological developments which greatly impacted post-war climbing. Before, pitons and carabiners were expensive and rare; ropes were still fashioned from natural fibers, bulky and prone to snap during long falls. "The leader must not fall" was the incontrovertible dictum that all climbers observed if they wanted anything but a short career. World War II changed all this with the plentiful supply of surplus army pitons, light-weight aluminum carabiners, and most importantly, strong and light nylon ropes.

For the next 20 years, standards rose steadily in both England and the United States. English climbers maintained their anti-piton stance and developed anchoring techniques which used runners over natural rock spikes, plus the wedging of pebbles—and eventually machine nuts slung with slings—as chockstones in cracks. Not surprisingly, the

English also pushed standards of boldness. They had little choice, for their protection was often dicey, at best. European standards were consolidated but, with their continued emphasis on attaining Alpine summits, actual rock climbing standards advanced little outside some exploring of large boulder summits in an area outside Paris. European manufacturers did, however, develop new nylon ropes that were stronger and much easier to handle.

By the early 1960s specialized rock climbing shoes appeared that were in appearance not totally different from what is available today: the Varappe, essentially a tennis shoe upper with a smooth rubber sole. These, in England and France, and the improved design of pitons in America, spurred standards in those respective areas. In the Americas and in England rock climbing was pretty firmly established as a specialized sport, and routes that led, say, merely to a cliff feature or to rappel points in the middle of blank cliffs were commonly done and respected. Sparingly in America, but increasingly in England climbers formulated strong aesthetic distinctions between using pitons and artificial aids to pull up on and using such anchors solely to protect the climbing of the cliff with hands and feet. This latter practice became known as free climbing. Styles and techniques remained largely provincial until the mid '60s, however; few climbers travelled widely to sample various climbing areas.

This changed dramatically by 1970, due in large part to the innovative development of rock climbing techniques born in California's Yosemite Valley (during the late '50s and through the '60s) which allowed the ascent of the spectacular cliffs there. To learn the piton aid techniques that enabled these ascents—and in splendid weather at that—climbers from around the world traveled to Yosemite. While they learned the American techniques, they also left as an heritage their own different approaches. By the early 1970s, American and English climbers completely dominated the development of the sport, and methods and equipment for climbing rock were becoming homogenized. Americans pitched the clunkier boots they had generally favored and adopted sensitive French and English smooth-soled shoes; in addition, the destructive and strenuous American pitoning techniques used in scaling the big cliffs were found to be less effective for free climbing than the gentler English nutting techniques. Moreover, innovative Americans started redesigning and commercially producing light and effective protection devices: First, aluminum nuts, then spring-loaded camming units. Simultaneously, rope manufacturers had been fine-tuning and improving the proper balance between strength, energy-absorbing stretch, and durability which led to a much more relaxed attitude toward falling.

By 1980, many climbers were traveling the world over to explore different areas, and climbers from many countries were involved in pushing standards. While the best climbers now trained exclusively for climbing, and the techniques and equipment were common to all, a new, pure gymnastic approach was applied to the style of ascent, particularly by the French. While this did not change the way that most climbers climbed, it resulted in further fundamental shifts from the roots of rock climbing as simply one of a number of skills necessary to gain the top of alpine peaks. Today's best rock climbers often "climb" the hardest routes by first descending the cliff to pre-arrange their protection and inspect the route for available holds. The subsequent ascent may take days, even weeks of repeated falls, all to the goal of climbing the route—now an extremely complicated gymnastic routine—straight through without falls. This approach has further led to the development of a formal competitive circuit, where climbers compete against the clock and each other on manmade and often indoor artificial climbing walls. To the average climber, however, sport climbing remains an exciting means to explore the natural world and enjoy the choreography of ascent—outside any arena.

RATING THE DIFFICULTY

Because the vast majority of your climbing will follow established routes already rated for difficulty and recorded in a guidebook, it is the following class system you will, with time, need to understand. It is your only yardstick as to how difficult a given climb is, and for this reason, it is both simple and comprehensive. The American rating system that follows is one of many in use around the world, as the chart on the next page explains.

CLASS
   1. Walking.
   2. Hiking. Mostly on established trails. Perhaps slogging along a stream bed.
   3. Scrambling. Angle is steep enough where hands are used for balance. A handline is rarely used, even for inexperienced climbers.
   4. Climbing risky enough that a fall could be fatal. Pulling with your arms required. A rope, some equipment, and protection techniques are used by most mountaineers.
   5. Technical rock climbing, commonly called "free climbing". A rope, specialized equipment and techniques are *always* used to protect against a fall. Fifth class climbing is the subject of *How to Rock Climb!*.
   6. Rock so sheer or holdless that ascent by using hands and feet is impossible. The equipment is used directly to aid the ascent, hence the common usage names for class 6 climbing: artificial, direct aid, or simply, aid climbing. Recall the hoary image of the intrepid climber hammering his way up the rock, his weight suspended on a succession of creaky pins. Things have changed, but the old notion still best illustrates what aid climbing is all about.

It is commonly agreed that technical rock climbing starts at fifth class, and the bulk of this book will deal with fifth class climbing. Fifth class climbing varies from low angle slabs, where only the beginner will relish a rope to 140-degree finger cracks so extreme that world class climbers might fall 100 times before they succeed, if indeed they ever do. In the early 1950s, fifth class climbing was designated as "easy", "moderate", and "advanced". As climbers got better and the climbs harder, a decimal system was adopted to more accurately rate the levels of difficulty within the class.
Devised in the early 1930s by the Rock Climbing Section of the Sierra Club, this system is principally used as an *index*

WORLD RATING SYSTEMS

West German (UIAA)	American (Decimal)	British	British	Australian	East German (GDR)	French
	5.5	4a	vs			
	5.6	4b	vs			
5+	5.7	4c	hvs		VIIa	5a
6-	5.8	4c	hvs	16	VIIb	5b
6	5.9	5a		17		5c
6+	5.10a	5b	E1	18	VIIc	6a
7-	5.10b	5b	E1	19	VIIIa	6a
7	5.10c	5c	E2	20	VIIIb	6b
7	5.10d	5c	E2	21	VIIIc	6b
7+	5.11a	6a	E3	22	IXa	6c
8-	5.11b	6a	E3	23	IXb	6c
8	5.11c	6a	E4	24		7a
8	5.11d	6a	E4	25	IXc	7a
8+	5.12a	6b	E5	26	Xa	7b
9-	5.12b	6b	E5		Xb	7b
9-	5.12c	6b	E5	27	Xb	7c
9	5.12d	6c	E6	28	Xc	7c
9+	5.13a	6c	E6	29		8a
10-	5.13b	6c	E7	30		8a
10-	5.13c	7a	E7			8b
10	5.13d	7a	E8	31		8b
10+	5.14a	7a	E8	32		8b
11-	5.14b	7b	E8			8c
11-	5.14c	7b	E9	33		8c
11	5.14d	7c	E9			9a

Though ratings vary from one area to the next, the fifth class decimal system is pretty uniform throughout the U.S.: a 5.8 in Yosemite would most likely be rated 5.8 at Tahquitz Rock as well. Climbers rely on the rating system being consistent, lest they are misled by guidebooks and end up on climbs either too hard or too easy for their fancy. Once a climber travels to a foreign area, however, he must become fluent in another rating system, for every country has an individual method of rating the difficulty of rock climbs. The attending graph plots comparative difficulties relative to various national rating systems. It is reasonably accurate, but not unequivocal. All rating systems are open ended, but the differences in difficulty between various number or letter ratings vary from country to country. There are other differences also: the British system factors a seriousness appraisal into the rating which preceeds the standard technical rating. (E5 6a) Note that the seriousness ratings overlap each other considerably in relation to the difficulty rating, as represented in the chart by the dashed lines.

of difficulty. The original scale, 5.0 through 5.9, was intended at the time of its adoption to cover the whole range of humanly possible rock climbs, anything above 5.9 being regarded as impossible. Standards are made to fall, of course, and shortly that one did.

The decimal system ceased to be purely "decimal" when aggressive pioneer climbers sought to rate climbs harder than established 5.9s; like other rating systems used throughout the world, the decimal system has evolved into an open-ended system that now includes climbs from 5.0, the easiest, to 5.14, to date, the most difficult leads achieved. Climbs of 5.10 through 5.14 are in the realm of the expert, and to better shade the nuances of these advanced levels, the letters a, b, c, and d were tacked onto the rating. For example, 5.12d represents the extreme end of the 5.12 standard, whereas a 5.12a or 5.12b is "easier", low end 5.12.

Sixth class, direct aid climbing is divided into five rating classes: A1 through A5, depending on the difficulty of placing protection anchors and their precariousness when placed. Put figuratively, this means you can hang your van from an A1 placement, but falling on a tenuous A5 thread of bashies will surely result in a harrowing hundred-foot zipper.

GRADES

The decimal system tells us how difficult a climb is. The attending grade rating tells us how much time an experienced climber will take to complete a given route.

Grade
  I.   One to three hours.
 II.   Three to four hours.
III.   Four to six hours. A strong half day.
 IV.   Full day. Emphasis on full.
  V.   One to two days. Bivouac is usually unavoidable.
 VI.   Two or more days on the wall.

The decimal rating is a relatively objective appraisal of difficulties, usually arrived at through consensus. The grade rating is posited as objective, but it uses the theoretical "experienced climber" as the example of how long a given route should take. Compare the grade rating with the par rating on a golf course. A par five means a honed golfer can probably hole the ball in five shots, rarely less, but a hacker will smile at a bogey six. Likewise, a world class team in top form can usually crank a grade V in one day, whereas the intermediate climber had best come prepared to spend the night.

FREE CLIMBING

There are two types of individuals who climb without a rope: the world-class climber whose experience is extensive, who knows his capabilities and limits perfectly, and the sorry fool who doesn't know any better and is courting disaster. More will be said on this topic in the leading chapter but let it be clear that, with rare exceptions, a rope and equipment are *always* employed in modern fifth class climbing. Accordingly, the layman often assumes that equipment directly assists a climber's ascent. It does, in the advanced realms of aid climbing, but not in the form known universally as free climbing.

Free climbing is the basis of all sport climbing, and can be loosely defined as upward progress gained by a climber's own efforts—using hands and feet on available features—unaided, or "free" of the attending ropes, nuts, bolts and pitons, which are employed only as back-up in case of a fall. These "features", the irregularities on the rock—cracks, edges, aretes, dihedrals, flakes—provide the climber his means for ascent. The variety is endless, and even uniform cracks of the same width have many subtle differences. It is precisely this fantastic diversity that gives climbing its singular challenge, where each "route" up the rock is a mental and physical problem-solving exercise whose sequence and solution are unique. Every climb is different, so discovering what works, for what climb and for what person, is the process that keeps the choreography of ascent fresh and exciting.

But it's not all ad-lib. There are numerous fundamental principles that apply to all climbing. The smooth coordination of hands and feet that allows fluid movement, balance, agility, and flexibility is a better weapon against gravity than brute strength. Endurance is generally more important than raw power. Preservation of strength is accomplished by keeping your weight over your feet, rather than hanging from your arms, and the best execution of any climb is that which requires the least effort. Finally, staying relaxed is half the battle. Much of climbing is intuitive, and the moves come naturally to the relaxed mind. However, climbing requires certain techniques that are inobvious and must be learned and practiced before you can hope to master them. Climbing is one of the most primal activities a person can undertake but, unlike Java Man, the modern climber usually wears shoes.

Featuring...

ARETE: an outside edge or corner of rock, perhaps as large as a mountain ridge.

BUTTRESS: much broader than an arete, a buttress is definitely mountain-size.

CHICKENHEAD: a bulbous knob of rock.

CHIMNEY: a crack of sufficient size to accept an entire body.

DIHEDRAL: an inside corner, formed by two planes of rock.

HEADWALL: a much steeper section of a cliff, residing towards the top.

HORN: a flake-like projection of rock, generally of small size.

LINE: the path of the route, usually the line of least resistance between other major features of the rock.

RIB: a narrow buttress, not so sharp as an arete.

ROOF/CEILING: a section of rock that extends out above your head like a...

SLAB: a section of rock of gentle angle, sometimes a relative reference when it's part of a vertical wall.

Rock Shoes

For your first couple of outings, snug-fitting tennis shoes will suffice, but try and rent a pair of rock shoes if possible. Many mountain shops and guide schools have rental gear. The special shoes make the experience much more enjoyable and considerably easier for a beginner. Should you choose to pursue climbing, your first purchase should be a pair of shoes. Most cost over 100 dollars, but can be resoled as they wear out, perhaps after 75 days of climbing.

Rock shoes have steadily evolved from the days of clunky boots, and with the advent of "sticky rubber" soles in 1982, the new shoes are so effective that many old timers claim it is "cheating" to use them. The old timers should know since they were the first to buy them. Built on orthopedically perfect lasts, with a glove-like yet bearable fit, they are a remarkable innovation. Since there are at least fifty brands currently available—with a host of particular features—choice for the beginner is mainly a matter of price and fit. For the expert, the choice is usually an attempt to match a specialized shoe to a particular kind of rock or a specific technique. Some shoes are stiffer, good for standing on minuscule footholds, but not so good for pure friction. There are shoes for cracks, for limestone "pocket" climbing, and those designed to fit inside insulated high altitude boots; in short, an expert will often have a whole quiver of boots for various applications, much as a champion skier will have various skis for different conditions and uses.

A beginner can get confused, but each manufacturer has a generic, all-around boot best suited for the novice. Since a beginner's footwork is generally poor, he will trash his boots

CLIMBING SHOES

(from left to right) The 5.10 Vertical, a great multipurpose shoe, particularly good for crack climbing; Dolomite Edlinger, low-cut and light, stiff at the toe, and made for steep face and pocket climbing; Asolo Opera, typical of the light slipper, sensitive and feather light.

much faster than an experienced climber, so you might consider buying the cheapest pair you can find, at least for that first pair. While a "general use" boot is probably the novice's most practical choice, you will eventually want the boot best suited to the type of climbing you prefer. For lower angle face climbing, a soft sole and a supple upper is best. For steep wall or pocket climbing, you'll want a tight fitting boot with good lateral support and a three-quarter height upper—for ankle flexibility. Climbing magazines routinely have an equipment review which rates the relative merits of each brand's wares. Remember, however, that despite amazing advances in both rubber and boot construction, there's no magic in boots: the key is knowing how to use them.

Climbers have traditionally worn boots which are uncomfortably snug because the boots rarely fit correctly, and you compensated by forcing your foot to fit the boot. If you didn't, your foot would rotate inside the boot when standing on small holds. Modern climbing shoes are constructed on anatomically correct lasts, contoured to fit your foot, thus eliminating the torture of undersized boots. Some brands may favor a wider or narrower last, so try on an assortment of different boots until you find the perfect fit. It is more important to your climbing to have a good fitting boot than one that is specifically designed for the type of climbing you want to do. The foot should not rotate in the boot; neither should the toes be painfully curled in the toe box. Most climbers wear their boots with thin socks; others prefer no socks, citing better sensitivity and comfort, though after a time their boots tend to take on a certain rare bouquet. Try it both ways. A floppy pair of boots is frustrating to climb in, and you don't want to spend upwards of 100 dollars and waste all the technology on a sloppy fit. Most climbing shops have rentals so you can feel how the boots perform before plopping down a c-note.

An alternative to proper boots are the new "slippers", which resemble snug, bedroom slippers, with a sticky sole. For the veteran whose feet are chronically sore after a decade of cramming them into undersized boots, these slippers are a boon, for they work surprisingly well and are very comfortable. They do require strong feet, but make for a sensitivity on rock not inherent in regular boots. However, on most climbs slippers definitely *underperform* a proper boot, so beginners, who need every advantage available, might do well to stick with a normal rock shoe—for that first season, anyway.

Dirt, grime, oil, tree sap, and such can dramatically effect a sole's performance, so always keep your boots clean, and limit walking around in them to a minimum. Most climbing soles are not rubber at all, but T.D.R.—Thermo Dynamic Rubber—a petroleum-based synthetic. Regardless, the T.D.R. oxidizes and hardens just like rubber, and though this is only a surface condition it can affect performance on all but the so-called "Stealth" rubbers. An occasional wire brushing is the solution for both grime and hardening. Hot car trunks loosen the glue bonds of the rands and soles. Super Glue can fix this, but it's better to avoid excessive heat. Foot powder helps avoid stitch rot from sweaty feet.

Chalk

The use of carbonate of magnesium—or gymnastic chalk—to soak up finger and hand sweat, is one of climbing's ethical issues, and arguments pro and con are continually waged, as they should be. The advantage is that chalk increases your grip, plain and simple. On coarse sandstone, in 40-degree shade, the advantages are minimal, if any. But stick a climber on a greasy, glacier-polished Yosemite crack in mid-summer swelter and his hands will sweat like he's going to the electric chair—and chalk can make a huge difference. The arguments against chalk are many, almost all true. The golden rule for all climbers is respect for the environment: You leave the place as you found it. Though not permanent, excessive chalk build-up is not only an eyesore, it telegraphs the sequence of holds to subsequent teams, diminishing the factor of discovery so vital to the climber's experience. Also, too much chalk on the holds can make the grip worse than no chalk at all, a common condition that has caused some climbers to carry a toothbrush to uncake chalky holds. Knowing that an afternoon thundershower usually returns the rock to pristine status, and in light of the real advantage chalk affords, chalk has generally become an accepted evil the world over. But there are exceptions. On cliffs so steep rain never touches them, any chalk will be there until Jesus comes home. For this, and other reasons, some areas have, through consensus, decided chalk will not be tolerated, and visiting climbers should respect the local custom.

Several manufacturers have begun making chalk in colors, intending to match the color of local rock. Though the quality and effectiveness of this chalk is poor, time will eventually find the right chemistry, and the day when the cliffside is not peppered in white paw marks will one day come.

Helmets

In pure rock climbing areas like Yosemite, Colorado's Eldorado Canyon, Tahquitz rock in California, or the Gunks of upstate New York, you can climb for years and never see anyone wearing a helmet. The reason is that in these areas, rockfall is rare, and while it is possible to injure your head in a fall, for some reason it rarely happens. Climbers have accordingly avoided wearing helmets because they feel awkward. However, in the mountains, where the terrain is often anything but glacier-polished granite or dense sandstone, it's only the certified madman who doesn't wear a helmet. It's your choice. If you feel better wearing a helmet, do so.

Climbing Skills: The Face

Picture a climber on a steep wall of orange sandstone. Above her, the rock sweeps up like a cresting wave, without a single crack to lodge her hands or feet in. From our point of view, there appear to be no holds at all, just a polished wall; yet she moves steadily up—high stepping, counter balancing, reaching, ever fluid and graceful. She's face climbing, and to the beginner it looks harrowing. But you'll soon learn that face climbing is the most natural form in all the climbing game. It varies from low angle slabs, where balance and the friction of good boots are all that's required, to 120-degree overhanging test-pieces where Conanesque strength is essential to even get off the ground.

The first rule in face climbing is to keep your weight over your feet. We live much of our lives on our feet, better suited for load bearing than the arms, which tire quickly regardless of their strength. Keeping your weight over your feet is the result of *correct body position*. On face climbs less that 90 degrees (or dead vertical), the body should remain in the same upright posture as when you're walking on level ground. The reasons are these: First, the vertical posture is the only one that is naturally balanced. If you've ever balanced a stick on your finger, you'll remember it is only possible when the stick is vertical. Second, when your body is vertical, gravity forces your weight straight down onto your boots, which is best for maximum friction and purchase. A beginner's initial reflex, to hug the rock, may feel more secure, but this only throws the whole body out of balance; and when all the unbalanced weight is transferred to the feet, the boots tend to skate off. Lastly, when the body is vertical, the climber's face is not plastered against the rock and his field of vision is open to see how to proceed. So stand up straight, stay in balance, and keep your weight over your feet.

Correct body position is standing with weight over the feet.

FOOTWORK

Except for overhanging rock, you will climb basically on your feet, the arms only acting as a support mechanism to stay in balance as you step up from one foothold to the next. It is almost magical how well the new sticky boots adhere; but even so, a beginner will take some time before learning to trust his feet. Once you realize that the boots do indeed stick, you can begin exploring the various ways to stand on holds. The variety of different foot holds encountered is virtually infinite, but there are basically three different variations of standing on one: by pure friction, by edging, and by smearing.

Friction

To use the friction step is to simply choose the best spot, place your foot, and balance on up. You will generally want to get as much of the sole over as much surface area as possible, thus increasing the friction co-efficient. Much of the art comes from one's ability to choose just the right place to step, having a keen eye for any irregularities, rough spots, or indentations. Even the most flawless face usually has slight ripples; and above these ripples is a lower-angled spot—if only a single degree less than the mean angle—and the experienced climber scours the face for these. In smaller dishes and scoops, the heel is kept rather high when pure frictioning, for this increases the frontal pressure on the sole. On more uniform slopes, a lowered heel puts the relatively wide rubber under the ball of the foot to the rock. Try it both ways.

The Friction Step

Perhaps more than in any other type of climbing, keeping your weight correctly balanced over your feet is absolutely essential in friction climbing. A good exercise is to get on a slab and, starting from the upright posture, slowly lower your torso closer to the rock. You will immediately learn that the closer you get to the rock, the less your boots will stick. Different rock has different friction properties. Polished limestone is desperate even at 45 degrees; but the coarse quartz monzonite at Joshua Tree allows pure friction well into the 70-degree realm; and given some supporting hand holds, the friction step can be useful even on overhanging rock. Discovering just how steep an angle you can friction up and picking the optimum foot placements is a function of experience, but as with all face climbing, friction climbing is natural and readily learned.

Edging

The practice of placing the very edge of the boot on any hold which is clear-cut—the serrated edge of a flake, a cluster of crystals, a pronounced wrinkle—is called edging. The word "edge" applies not only to the boot's running edge, but also to the "edge" which forms the top of the hold. You usually edge when the hold is sharp. The edge of the boot is placed directly on the hold and the sole finds purchase by conforming onto the rock once the boot has been weighted.

Edging is the most basic method of standing on holds, but it takes a lot of practice to become proficient.

We generally edge with the inside of the boot, near the outside of the big toe. Both your foot and most modern boots are designed to stand most easily on this section of the boot. Also, when edging on dime-sized edges, it is necessary to feel just how good or bad the boot is holding, and the area around the big toe is the most sensitive and best suited for this. However, it is not unheard of for people to prefer edging off the ball of the foot, and many times it is necessary to edge with the boot pointing straight on the hold. Toe-in edging, as in small pockets, requires strong toes to provide rigidity and control and is not a prefered technique, though commonly required on limestone and various volcanic crags. While we normally climb directly facing the rock, many times you will find it necessary to step one leg inside the other, particularly when traversing. Knowing how to edge with the outside of the boot is essential here. Outside edging is almost always done just back from the origin of the small toe. The foot's bone structure makes that section of the foot fairly rigid as opposed to the rest of the outside part of the foot, which is fleshy and flexible, and which gives the boot edge every reason to "butter off" the hold.

Edging is an exercise in precision. Many edges are so small they can't even be seen until you're at them. Careful placement of the foot is essential, and once the boot is weighted, it is likewise essential not to change the attitude of the boot lest you pop off. Thus, one key to proficient face climbing lies in learning to isolate the movements of your legs and upper body from the rigidity of your foot placement. Contrary to common sense, a razor sharp boot edge is not ideal for standing on small holds. Because rubber stretches once weighted, a slightly rounded edge is less likely to "buttress" or fold off the small foothold. Most shoes feature a sole which is bevelled back underfoot, resulting in more stable edging and less "buttressing".

Edge holds will appear at all kinds of different angles, and it is not the norm that an edge is chiseled perfectly for a foothold. For this, the edge of the boot must be applied to the foothold at the angle of the hold, which requires ankle flexibility, and that angle must be maintained while your weight is on it. In the case of extreme edging, when the holds are very small indeed, many of the edges are "time-bomb" in nature, meaning the climber cannot "camp" on them too long without the boot "blowing off" from either toe fatigue or the fact that even the best boot cannot stick to marginal holds indefinitely. More will be discussed about this in the chapter: The Art of Leading.

Edging, using the outside of the right foot and the normal edging area of the left.

Smearing

Smearing is the technique of standing on rounded holds. You stand on a smear hold as though it was an edge, but it is the friction of the applied boot sole, rather than the boot's edge, which affords the purchase. Many times the foot is smeared not on, but over the hold, because once weighted, it is slowly but surely melting off. Likewise, sharp but miniscule holds on a lower angled slab might be more securely smeared than edged, combining smear tactics with the friction step. In the era of the hard-soled rock shoes, particularly when many rock shoes had cleated soles, smearing was a risky practice, rarely done; with the new sticky rubber soles, smearing has become a common means of using ill-defined footholds.

Tricks and General Technique

The technique of footwork is one of subtle precision and is tough to explain, let alone illustrate; but if you understand the principles, practice will bring to light what good technique can do for you. The problem with most climbers is that they rush things. They hug the rock, their feet are kicked towards, not placed on, the holds, and because they don't

Heel hooked overhead, Paul Piana cranks out a bleak line of overhanging holds on "Desdichado" (5.13c), Eldorado Canyon, Colorado. In the absence of footholds, the heel hook can act as a third arm, easing the strain on beleaguered fingers.

Beth Wald photo

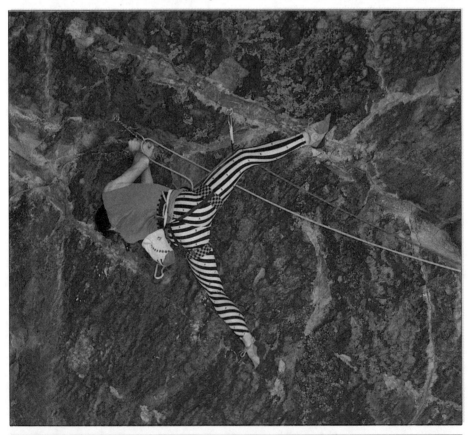

trust their boots, their limbs quake and their boots are often skidaddling all over. You've got to settle in and relax. The frantic climber is the first to make a mistake, to miss a key hold. You must choose your holds carefully and always follow the line of least resistance. This sometimes means passing a good hold which is off to the side and would require awkward, more difficult moves to get to. Maintaining balance often means using smaller steps and smaller holds rather than awkward, off-balance strides between larger holds. The climber must move methodically and with precision, placing his feet carefully, staying balanced, and easing up onto doubtful holds, rather than jumping upon them. The aim is to climb smoothly and gracefully, and to use as little energy as possible. A good rule is whenever you reach a good hold, pause and compose yourself. Learn to stand on the heel of your boot when the chance arises. This takes the strain off the calves and puts it onto the skeletal system, which never tires.

Sloppy footwork is generally the result of impatience and fear. If this problem seems insurmountable, practice on slabs low to the ground, get used to standing on marginal holds, keeping your weight over your feet. Experiment and learn. Traverse along the base of the cliff, where a fall means slipping four inches to the ground, and where you can try even the most improbable sequences. Practice walking over little slabs with no hands. Always aim to climb precisely, fluid and relaxed. Striving to meet goals of control, rather than for success at all costs, will help build good technique. And always fight the initial instinct to only look up for holds. Many times the beginner will look down only to gauge the distance he is above the ground. You must pay attention to the climbing at hand. If you watch an experienced climber, you'll quickly see at least half the time he is looking down at his feet, scanning for holds, and placing them with keen eyes.

Heel Hooking

Heel hooking is the attempt to use the foot as a hand and is rarely used on climbs less than vertical. Basically, you hook the heel of your boot over or behind a flake, knob, corner, or any feature that will accommodate such a move. Most often, the foot is actually kicked over the head and hooked over a shelf or ledge. You then pull with the foot, folding the chest in and up until you can reach the hooked hold. A heel hook is often a way to avoid throwing a strenuous and risky dynamic move; and in isolated cases, a climb is impossible without using this technique. Though it is sometimes possible, even necessary to hook something other than the heel—the toe, perhaps—try not to hook anything above the shoe's rand (the strip of rubber that circles the boot above the sole). The rand is usually made from the same compound as the sole and grabs the rock

Torque between the toe and heel placed in a hole or horizontal crack below an overhang can keep the body from swinging out and provide stability and reach.

well, whereas the leather upper is prone to skate off even a jagged flake.

When lateral movement is required on steep climbs, the body will often feel like it's set to hinge out and away from the face. Climbers often look for a side hold or flake at, or below waist level to hook a heel on, thus holding the body in place while the hands are arranged on other holds. Heel hooking requires good flexibility and moxie. The applications and variations are many, but it's normally a technique to employ a "third arm", or to stay in balance where otherwise it would be impossible.

HANDHOLDS

There seem to be as many different kinds of holds as there are ways to grab them, but there remain five basic techniques: The open grip; the cling, or "crank" grip; the vertical grip; the pocket grip; and the pinch grip. Again, as with footwork, a calm and deliberate manner, coupled with feeling different ways of using the hold, will result in added confidence that you are getting maximum performance from the hold.

The OPEN GRIP is the way you latch either a big hold or a rounded hold. Your fingers conform to the natural curvature of the hold and you pull. The notion is to grab the best section of the hold, and the climber should feel around for the most secure position rather than just pulling straight-away the moment the hand is placed. With big holds, this is not so important; but when a hold is both small and rounded, the slightest shift in hand and finger position can make a huge difference.

With the open grip, the hand functions like a claw. The forearm muscles fight the tendency of the fingers to straighten out, but what supplies the actual purchase is the friction of the finger pads on the hold. Accordingly, you try and cover the most surface area possible, increasing the friction at the power point. As with any hand hold, if the hold is too small to accommodate all your fingers, give priority to the strongest digits, starting with the index finger, on down to the pinky.

Experts in bio-mechanics insist that the open grip is least stressful on both joints and tendons and should be used whenever possible. The one drawback with the open grip is that on severely rounded holds, the forearm muscles work overtime to keep the fingers from straightening out, and if the climber hangs too long, the forearms are sure to get "torched".

The CLING GRIP (aka "CRANK" or "CRIMP" grip) is used most commonly on flat-topped holds, be they minute edges, or half-inch-sized shelves. The fingers are bent at the second knuckle and the thumb is wrapped over the index finger if possible. Sometimes the thumb is braced against the side of the index finger, but whatever position the thumb

1. The Open Grip
2. The Cling Grip
3. The Cling Grip, with the use of a thumb to reinforce the fingers.

ends up in, it's your best friend as it's considerably stronger than any of your fingers.

The cling grip works much like a boot does when edging. Once weighted, the fingers dig into the rough contours of the hold.

As a result, and because the second knuckle is locked off, you can apply an amazing amount of torque to a hold using the cling grip. You can also shred your finger tips on sharp edges, and the world class climber can incur finger injuries owing to the sharp angle the tendons make and the stress the knuckles absorb. Regardless, the cling grip is far and away the chosen technique when clasping sharp holds.

Some experts claim the cling grip is a natural posture, but most beginners find it otherwise. It's a foreign configuration, and it takes time for the knuckles to get accustomed to the stress. Because you don't want the fingers to rip off the rock, you'll feel around for the best part of the hold, which might also be the most painful. Only practice can reveal exactly how this all works, but you've got the basic notion.

The VERTICAL GRIP involves bending the first and second knuckle and pulling straight down on the hold, oftentimes with one's fingernails behind the tiniest of edges. This grip is used exclusively on micro-flakes found on steep slab climbs, is painful, and has been said to be the climbing equivalent of "en pointe" in ballet.

The POCKET GRIP is most often used on limestone and volcanic rock, which is typically pocked with small holes. The ultimate form of the pocket grip is one finger stuck into a hole. Because it is rare that a pocket will accommodate all of one's fingers, the first choice is the strong middle finger, next the index finger, and so on. It is sometimes possible to stack the fingers on top of each other for increased torque. Be careful to feel the pocket for any jagged edges, which can cut into the finger. Also, keep the pull in line with the axis of the finger, not pulling side to side, which is like bending a hinge—your knuckle—the wrong way.

The PINCH GRIP is the action a lobster does with it's pincers, and what a climber does when pinching a knob, flute, rib, or other protuberance. Though self explanatory, a climber will often feel around quite a bit to find just where his thumb and fingers fit best. On small knobs, the most effective pinch combines the thumb with the side of the index finger. Few people outside the ranks of brick layers have much natural pinching strength. For the most part, it has to be developed.

In addition to these five different grips, there are two other basic techniques which are often called upon in face climbing, the mantleshelf and the undercling.

The Mantleshelf

The mantleshelf is the rock feature; the act of surmounting it is called mantling. Picture the youngster heaving himself up and onto the top of a wall, then standing upon it. This is the basic form. Mantling is often performed on large fea-

4. The Vertical Grip
5. The Pocket Grip
6. The Pinch Grip

tures such as shelves or knobs, but when the face offers only one hold, you might find yourself mantling—albeit gently —a mere pencil-width crease. The technique has four components. After placing both hands on the mantleshelf, inspect the shelf or hold for the best place to mantle on, usually the biggest, flattest spot. If the spot is left of your face, you'll mantle with your left hand, and if it's to your right, then you mantle with your right. The second step involves hoisting the body up high enough to enable cocking one or the other arm on the mantleshelf. To get this upward impetus, use available footholds to ease the requisite arm power. On steep mantles, it is important to get the torso as high as possible before cocking the arm. If the arm is cocked low, with your weight checked only by skeletal tension, it is very strenuous for the triceps to initiate upward thrust from this "bottomed out" position. The third part, the press, can be very strenuous, and often depends on the free hand pulling, plus a certain body English to get started. The concern is to make sure the palm doesn't skate off the shelf, a real possibility on a rounded or slick surface. Most climbers find the bottom, or "heel" of the palm is best suited for mantling. Once you have "pressed out" the mantle, try and find a hand hold above for the free hand. This makes it much easier to execute the last phase: the step up and leg press into the standing position. For balance, you'll want the foot close to the supporting hand. Often the hand must be moved to free up space for the foot. Using the knee is tempting here but only makes it more difficult to get into the standing position. Rock your weight from your mantling hand to over your raised foot and try to stand up smoothly, without jerking motions which can dislodge the foot.

In extreme cases, you must mantle using only your fingertips in the cling position, or perhaps with the thumb in a small divot. Many times you will step onto a hold different than the one you have "pressed out". Regardless, the basics remain the same: staying balanced, utilizing footholds, not getting stuck in the "bottomed out" position, avoiding use of the knee, finding a handhold above for the free hand, and a smooth step up are key functions with any mantle.

One element of mantling often used as a stablizing influence on slabs is called "palming". In it's usual form, you lean off a straight arm and palm that has been placed below and to the side of the torso. The palmed hold can often bear enough weight to allow you to reach up and above, or to shuffle your feet up onto higher holds, or both.

The Undercling

Anytime you grab a hold with your palm up, whether you have your fingers behind a flake, or you're grabbing the underside of a small roof or step in the rock, you are underclinging. The technique is often used as a balancing tactic until a free hand can reach above to a better hold. In it's pure form, it functions through the opposing pressures of the hand or hands pulling out from the hold under which you are clinging and the force which is directed onto your feet. The technique is absolutely intuitive and self explanatory, but the following points are often helpful.

On a full-blown undercling, where you must traverse

THE UNDERCLING:

1. Reach up to the hold.
2-3. Step up while exerting upward force on the undercling hold.
4. Make the reach above to other holds.

1.   2.   3.   4.

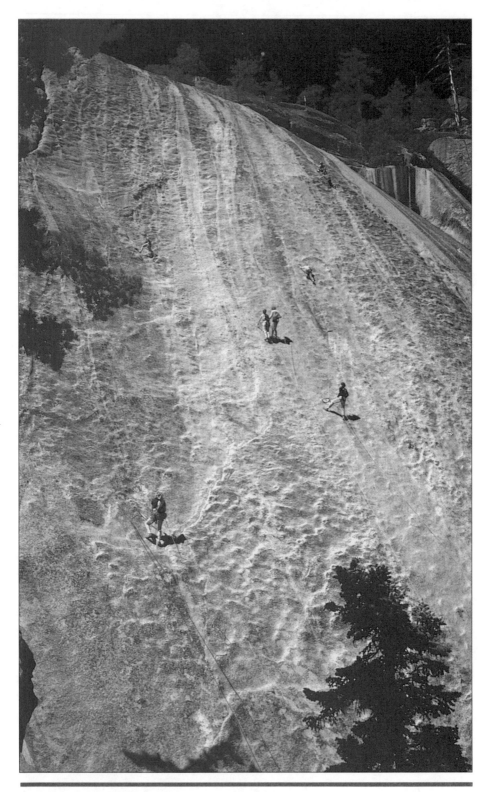

under a long flake, try and keep the arms straight, as this transfers some of the load off your biceps and deltoids and onto your bones. Utilize foot holds as much as possible to keep the load off your arms. Rather than undercling off the very tips of your fingers, try and get as much of your hand as possible behind the hold. Difficult underclings can involve lots of shuffling and cross-overs of both hands and feet. Only experience can show you the how and why of it all.

MOVEMENT: THE UPWARD FLOW

While we have discussed hands and feet separately, the aim of all climbing is to strive to have all the different moves blend into fluid upward movement. To look closely at different types of face climbing is the best way to understand the dynamics of this upward flow.

Slab Climbing

Slab climbing refers to smooth rock "slabs", usually ranging from 50 to 70 degrees. Beginning climbers are always startled to see a fine slab climber move over seemingly holdless rock. Slab climbing requires the application of every face climbing technique, frictioning here, palming there, edging, smearing, mantling. The ace slab climber is fluid and rarely stops lest he interrupt the rhythm of ascent. The body is kept well away from the rock, eyes ever scanning the rock for usable features, stopping when a good hold allows. A baseball player watches the ball all the way to where it meets the bat. Likewise, once a climber has chosen a hold, he watches his hand or foot all the way until he gains purchase. Because you can only watch one limb at a time, you only move one at a time. Keep this in mind and you will naturally assume the "tri-pod" position, maintaining at least three points of contact with the rock.

Because slabs are relatively low angle, climbing them is much more a process of balance and friction than of the brute strength required on steeper climbs. Consequently, slabs are a good place for a beginner to get accustomed to the nuances of footwork, body position, hand holds, and general movement.

While slab climbing is usually thought to be more fun than toil, there are exceptions. Extreme slab climbing occurs when the angle is too steep to just friction, yet the rock is devoid of holds—the classic "bald face". On these, balance, precision, unwavering concentration, and a dash of magic are most often your ticket to ride. "Micro-edging", often painful and always nerve wracking, is surely one of the most absorbing forms of climbing, for even the experienced expert is astonished just how small a hold it is possible to stand on. Unlike other forms of climbing, intricate sequences of movement are rarely necessary to ascend slab and friction climbs;

(page opposite)

Like gnats on a window-pane, three separate teams savor the fine slab climbing on the "Weeping Wall", Suicide Rock, California. Popular climbing areas like Suicide will find a host of climbers enjoying themselves on a given weekend. Because the routes take separate lines, the proximity may be close, the dangling banter as amusing as the climbing, but crossing paths is not a problem.

Bob Gaines photo

there are usually several ways to make upward progress, and this characteristic has led some climbers to label all slabs "boring".

Steep Face Climbing

Many of the recent strides in technical expertise are due to climbers venturing more and more onto the steep faces which past generations wrote off as either impossible or too contrived. Before the mid-seventies, a climbing route normally followed a prominent weakness or "line" up the cliff—a crack system, or an obvious dike or intrusion. As most of these natural lines were climbed, later generations, wanting the same notoriety and thrill of exploration that past climbers enjoyed, turned to the steep and often hold-bereft faces. No longer did climbers only seek out natural lines, but often chose the blankest, most difficult way up a cliff in their quest for the limits of technical difficulty.

But steep face climbs need not be extreme. Many are rife with big holds and ledges and are technically easier than difficult slabs. It's not the angle but the architecture and size of the holds that determines difficulty. However, steep face climbs, even if they have bulbous holds from bottom to top, are invariably more strenuous than lower angled climbs. They require much more from the arms, and in their most extreme expression, can involve hoisting the body up off one finger stuffed in a rounded pocket.

The overall strategy of climbing long and sustained steep faces will be discussed in greater detail in the chapter, The Art of Leading. For now, understand these basic principles: Unlike slab climbing, you will often see the steep face climber sucking his chest into the wall, trying to get the weight over his feet. Keeping the weight off the arms is tantamount to efficiently climbing steep faces, for you are often called on to make a strenuous upper body move, and if you've been needlessly hanging off your fingers, the strength might not be there when you most need it. The steeper the angle, the more the arms come into play; but try not to overpull, try to only hang on, and rely on the legs for upward thrust. It's often better to make two small moves than one long one. Try and avoid getting your body too stretched out, for this negates all your balance and is usually more strenuous. Avoid body positions that require Yogi-like contortions, and if you have to execute them, get into a more natural position quickly. And never pass up a good rest hold.

If you cannot find a decent foothold to snatch a breather, at least stop at the best hand hold and alternately shake the blood back into your lowered arm. As much as anything, the good steep face climber is the one who exerts the least energy, who figures out the most natural and easiest way to the top.

A beginner can benefit greatly by watching an expert climb, but in the case of steep face climbing, this can be misleading. The expert may appear to be, and may well be, sim-

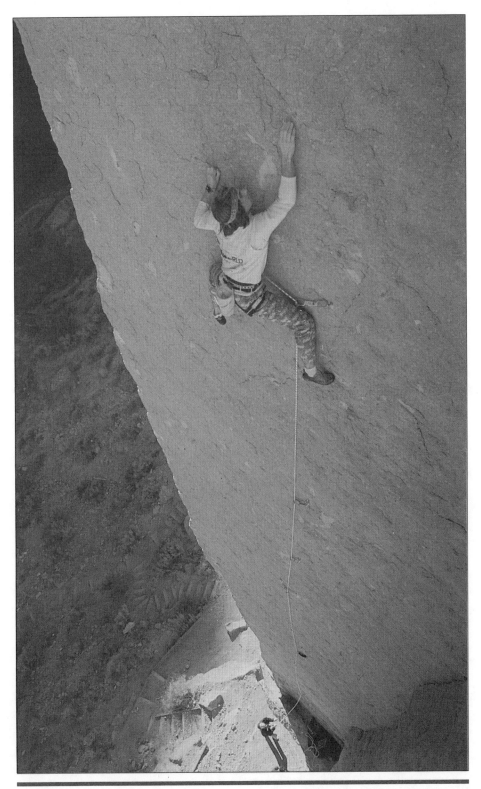

ply hauling himself up on his arms. What you might not know is that the expert climbs 300 days a year, has done so for a dozen years, has developed fantastic endurance and cardio-vascular strength and at the moment, he can't be bothered to fiddle with footholds. But put the same climber on a route at the very limit of his ability and you can bet your bottom dollar that he'll be observing the basic principles we've mentioned above. The reason is simple: The climber has not been born—nor will he be—who can hang indefinitely on his arms. Given enough stress, even the mightiest guns will "burn out".

Overhanging Face Climbing

While the realm of sustained, overhanging climbing is strictly the expert's turf, most climbing areas have moderate routes which feature an overhang, or a short overhanging section. In the Shawangunks in upstate New York there are numerous, moderate overhanging routes, moderate only because the holds are terrific, and the climb resembles swinging around on a big jungle gym. The technique does not differ radically from that required on steep faces, save that everything is more strenuous. Most all overhanging climbs go from one good hold to another. However, "good" here might only mean "not as bad" as the "bad" holds.

Climb the difficult stretches aggressively but not so fast to feel rushed. While you cannot get your weight directly over your feet, footwork on overhanging rock is probably more important than any other factor, for even the poorest foothold takes more weight off the arms than common sense would tell you. Try and keep your arms straight; when bent, the arms tire much faster. Ideally, the hands would act only as a hinge, holding your body to the wall as your legs push you upward. This is rarely possible, however. Try and avoid extremely long reaches for this requires the other arm to be locked off, and the locked off position, on overhanging ground, is probably the most strenuous position in all of climbing. When it is impossible to avoid locking off a hold, try and keep the hand close to the shoulder and the elbow close to your side. This is easily confirmed on a pull-up bar; try letting go with one hand and keeping your chin above the bar. You'll quickly realize your only chance is to assume the lock-off position just described. The geometry of the body makes it so. In rare instances on exceptionally arduous climbs, you might see a climber briefly locking off a hold well to one side of his body, and reaching up quickly to a hold on the other side. Be consoled that such a maneuver is limited to the very best and requires a degree of strength unusual in even world class climbers.

Dynamic Climbing

A dynamic move is another way to describe a lunge, where a climber vaults off a hold and is propelled to another.

Dynamic moves range from six-inch slaps to all-out jumps, where a climber is completely clear of the rock, before quickly clasping holds above, at the apex of his leap. Only a decade ago, dynamic moves were virtually unheard of on all but practice rocks. As climbs got more and more difficult, dynamics ("dynamos", or simply " 'mo's") became a requirement on many of the harder testpieces. Properly performed, dynamics are climbing's most athletic expression, requiring perfect coordination, raw power, and precise timing.

Usually, dynamic moves are "thrown" on overhanging rock to span long stretches between good holds. But not always. Sometimes dynamics are thrown from a poor hold to a pathetic hold. While it is very occasionally necessary to generate the thrust solely with the arms, with the feet dangling in space, dynamics are usually performed by an explo-

In flight! All limbs dislocated from the holds, Mike Paul slaps for the sloping top on "Saturday Night Live", a difficult dynamic boulder problem at Joshua Tree, California. Having generated momentum off lower holds, Mike must fly upward and stick a one-hand latch, not letting his lower body swing him off the top.

Gregg Epperson photo

sive pull from the arms while concurrently, the feet kick off footholds. Once the lunge is underway, one hand shoots up and slaps onto the hold for which you're lunging. Ideally, the climber takes advantage of the brief moment of weightlessness that occurs at the apex of the leap—the dead point—to place the hand with accuracy on the hold.

Sometimes a hold is too greasy or rounded to lock off and reach above, but while hanging below, it is possible to generate enough momentum to literally fly to that upper hold. This phenomenon is difficult to explain, but is obvious when you encounter it. Rounded holds, even on very overhanging rock, are often fairly secure when your arms are extended and your bulk is hanging directly below them. But the higher you pull up, the worse they become because your body position forces you to pull increasingly out, rather than down on the hold. For this reason, big dynamic moves are usually initiated with the arms fully extended.

This is the basic form of the intentional dynamic. Much more common is the dynamic thrown out of desperation, where a climber has worked himself into a compromising position, and just before peeling off, he slaps for a hold. Another situation is: You pull up statically to a certain height. There is a hold right above your face, but if you let go, you'll fall off. You let go with one hand and hope you can slap the hold faster than gravity takes you down.

There are many more examples of dynamics which one can discover for himself. Be certain to understand that only one climb in a hundred requires any dynamic climbing, and that the place to practice dynamics is not on a long climb, but inches off the ground.

CLIMBING SKILLS: CRACKS

The most visible and tangible weakness up a cliff is a large crack that runs from bottom to top. When you walk to the base of the rock and your partner asks where the climb is, there's no mystery to it. A climbing route is often referred to as a "line", a term derived from the line the crack forms on the cliff, but a good line doesn't necessarily follow a crack. It may pass over steep, otherwise featureless rock, be clean, offering exciting locations, great exposure, and a straight, or "plumb-line" topography. A "poor line" might wander all over a rubbly cliff, through vegetation, up dark and dripping recesses. But good or bad, a line is a route waiting to be climbed, if it hasn't already. A prominent crack system is nature's way of telling us where to climb and when expeditions are mounted to big, faraway cliffs, or when a beginner studies a crag for the first time, eyes naturally home in on any crack system the cliff affords. "That's a climb there", he'll say to himself.

While face climbing might be a natural movement, few face climbs follow natural lines, and while cracks are natural lines, crack climbing is a very unnatural enterprise. Crack climbing requires subtle and strenuous techniques where the only hope of mastery lies in experience. All crack climbing involves either jamming or torquing the limbs or body inside the crack.

There are two types of "jamming". With the classic "hand jam", the hand is placed in an appropriately sized crack, and the muscles expand the hand inside the crack. The various counter pressures result in a locked, or "jammed" hand, which can be very secure when properly placed. The second method involves torquing and camming the appendage in a bottleneck or constriction in the crack. In wide cracks, the limbs are often twisted or stacked; and in very wide cracks you find wedging and cross pressures are the only way up. No two climbers are exactly the same size, however, and where one climber might pull fist jams, another might get hand jams, and so on. Anyone with aspirations towards big, classic climbs will soon discover such routes predominantly follow crack systems.

The names and different techniques do not correspond to any fixed sized crack, but only refer to the method you must employ based on how your fingers or hands fit the crack as described. Climbers with extremely thin hands enjoy certain advantages, but this tends to even out in the long run.

FINGER JAMMING:
1. "Pinky lock"
2. and 3. Standard
   finger locks.
4. Off-size fingers

Finger Cracks

Finger cracks vary in width from shallow seams into which you can only get the tip of your pinky, to a crack which swallows all your fingers. Halfway between pure crack climbing and pure face climbing, thin cracks require techniques from both forms. Consequently, finger cracks are often technically demanding.

It is a very rare crack that is absolutely parallel-sided. Most cracks, thin and otherwise, vary in size, if only barely; and it's these constrictions that you look for. The knuckles are the thickest part of the finger, particularly the second knuckle. It is possible to jam the knuckles above constrictions in the crack, and when the wrist is bent and the arm pulls down, the knuckle becomes locked—the standard "finger lock". This practice may be as painful as it sounds, and it's crucial to first wiggle the fingers around to attain the best fit before you weight them. The fingers are usually inserted such that the thumb is down, but this can be varied depending on the situation.

Many times it is better to jam the shank of the finger—the fleshy section between knuckles. Find the appropriate slot, insert as many fingers as possible (hand in the thumb down position), then rotate the wrist downward. This will naturally create a camming torque on the stacked fingers. Remember that the thumb is stronger than your fingers, so always try and brace it against the index finger in whatever position feels best. This results in a sort of guy-wire effect which keeps the jam from rotating out.

For ultra-thin, less-than-first-knuckle cracks, you assume the thumbs-up position to utilize the thinnest digit—the pinky. "Pinky locks" are marginal jams at best, and function well only if the pull is straight down. Oftentimes a straight-in crack (a crack splitting a uniform face) requires a combination of thumbs-up and thumbs-down jamming; and when—climbing a crack in a corner, say—this combination is required, the lower hand is always in the thumb-up attitude.

When the constrictions are slight and the jams are loose or marginal, leaning to one side or the other will often add a degree of stability to the process. If the crack is off-set, where one side of the crack is raised above the other, the thumb can apply opposite pressure against the off-set edge.

Such are the basic positions for vertical cracks. But many thin cracks slant one way or another; and just as many snake around in the course of even a short climb. As the crack leans, your body will inevitably be below the crack, and this pretty well dictates that the upper hand will have to be kept in the thumb-down position, your lower hand in a thumb-up position. With leaning thin cracks, it is sometimes possible, even desirable, for the lower hand to be thumb-down. But to place the upper hand thumb-up means to crank against the knuckles *the wrong way*, since slanting thin cracks are usually a combination of jamming, and pulling down on the lower edge of the crack.

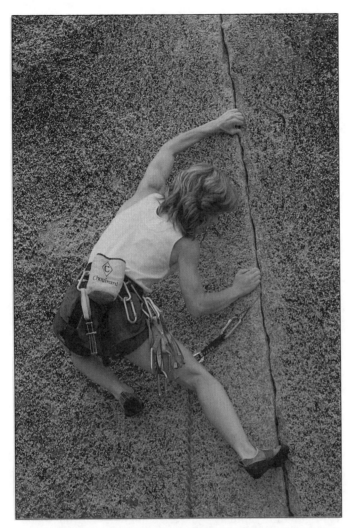

No buccaneer, svelte Lynn Hill, one of the world's great free climbers, smears, edges, liebacks, and clings up the "Pirate" (5.12), Suicide Rock, California. Too thin to jam, too bald to face climb, the climb requires creative face and crack combinations to succeed. On such difficult routes, confusing postures and withering fatigue may so vex the leader that performing the winning sequence may come only after dozens of falls and days of effort, if at all.

Greg Epperson photo

No one can climb a thin crack without feet. Even the best jams pump the arms quickly, and without good footwork, you're lost. Like face climbing, thin cracks are usually a matter of finding the hand positions which best support the upper body, while your legs supply the upward thrust. Thin cracks get progressively more difficult as the footholds disappear. Always scan the face for footholds. Thin cracks are strenuous, so never pass a rest spot, even if you're not tired. Leaning off the jams puts the climber to one side of the crack. If there's a foothold on that side, use the outside edge of the upper foot on that hold, for it keeps you more balanced, in a far less twisted attitude. Thin cracks occasionally open up and allow a flared "toe-jam". Most rock boots feature low profile toes tapered particularly for this. Twist the ankle and get the sole of the boot vertical, then jam the toe in above the constriction; and try not to move it once weighted. When there are no footholds and no pockets for toe jams,

OFF-HAND CRACKS

1-3. The thumb stack

climbers will sometimes stick the outside edge of the boot vertically in the crack. Though this is marginal, it works surprisingly well, for it creates a foothold, and invariably takes some weight off the arms. The last choice is to simply use friction, with the sole flat against the rock.

Save for a substantial shelf to stand on, "stem" holds are a thin crack climber's best friend. These are holds, one on each side of the crack, which slant in, and on which the climber can "stem", or bridge his feet. A good stem provides a solid base for the lower torso and often allows the climber to shake out a tired hand, sometimes both hands. On a steep thin crack, you hope for two good finger locks within reach. Keeping the arm extended (remember, a bent arm tires quickly), suck the chest in and get your weight over your feet. Shake out one arm at a time until you've recovered enough to carry on.

When climbing thin cracks in corners, it is often possible to stem between the two walls using pure friction. If you find a stem hold, look to paste one foot in the corner, and "backstep" the outside foot onto the stem hold.

All these descriptions may sound straightforward, but climbing a thin crack rarely is. The best solution is usually a subtle blend of all these techniques. The correct sequence is rarely obvious, requiring patience and a certain amount of feeling about to discover what best works for you. Hasty moves can result in painful abrasions, so climb fluidly. We have effectively broken down the variety of individual moves likely to be encountered on thin cracks. Putting these moves together, with tips on strategy and approach for all crack climbing, will be taken up in the chapter: The Art of Leading.

Off-Hand Cracks

An off-hand crack is too big for the fingers and too small for the hand, where the third knuckle butts into the crack and the fingers rattle around inside. Cracks this size rarely allow good toe jamming—just a tad too thin—so you're doubly cursed. Everything's wrong about this size, and there are no easy solutions. One way to approach the problem is to keep the fingers straight and together and stuff then into the hilt, thumb-up. You lever the fingertips off one side of the crack and the back of the fingers—or knuckles—off the other side—sort of a crow-bar effect. This "bridge" jam is terrifically strenuous and difficult. Another way is to insert the hand thumb-down, overlap the middle finger over the index, overcrank with your wrist, and pray that it doesn't rip out. Far and away the best method is the "thumb-stack". Place the thumb near the outside of the crack, the first knuckle against one side, the thumb pad against the other. (For this to work effectively, the crack must be thinner than the link of jammed thumb. The thumb is inserted at an angle, the pad higher than the knuckle) Curl the fingers over the thumb nail and pull down, effectively wedging, through downward pressure, the thumb between the two walls. At first this technique feels strange and impossible, but with practice it's really the only viable technique.

Because off-hand jams are always cammed or torqued, they're invariably less secure than a good finger lock. Hence, footwork is key. If you are lucky, the crack will open up enough to allow at least marginal toe jams. If not, you're essentially face climbing with your feet. If there are no face holds, your world is a pretty grim place.

Hand Cracks

Most climbers think hand cracks are the last word in crack climbing. The crack is perfectly suited for both hands and feet, the technique is readily learned and very secure, and vertical, even overhanging hand cracks are often reasonable. An added boon is that—for reasons only a geologist can guess—hand cracks often bisect spectacular sections of rock, and many of the world's classic climbs involve extensive hand jamming.

Hand jamming is usually done with straight fingers, bent at the palm, or third knuckle. The thumb-up hand jam is a tri-pod configuration, with the fingertips and heel of the palm on one side of the crack, and the back of the hand and knuckles on the other. Some climbers like to fold the thumb in across the palm; just as many like to bridge the thumb off the index finger. Whatever thumb position you choose, it's the expanding action of the hand that creates the actual jam, which when properly performed, is the most powerful jam of all. Once mastered, an experienced climber will often prefer to hang off a "bomber" hand jam than off an equally good shelf.

When climbing straight-in hand cracks, most climbers prefer the thumb-up position, though there's no reason the thumb-down jam isn't as good. When the crack jags, or is a little slim, the thumb-down jam is normally—but not always—employed. With the thumb-up jam, the wrist is straight. The wrist twists with the thumb-down jam, and the result is a torquing action that can sometimes add power to a thin or bottoming jam.

With slanting hand cracks, you will generally jam the upper hand thumb-down. When you find it necessary to lean off the crack, the top hand is invariably thumb-down, the bottom hand thumb-up. There are exceptions to these examples, and climbing even the most peerless, straight-in hand crack may require all these techniques, if only to vary the stress and to use other muscles. A hand jam is often tight, and the back of the hand is frequently set against coarse rock. Serious abrasions can result from hasty jamming, or rotating the hand in the crack—which is a common mistake as you pull up and past a poor or insecure jam. To avoid this, place the jam so the fingers are pointing straight into the crack. As you pull up, rotate your wrist—not your hand—keeping the jam locked tight.

With hand cracks, which readily accept feet, turn your

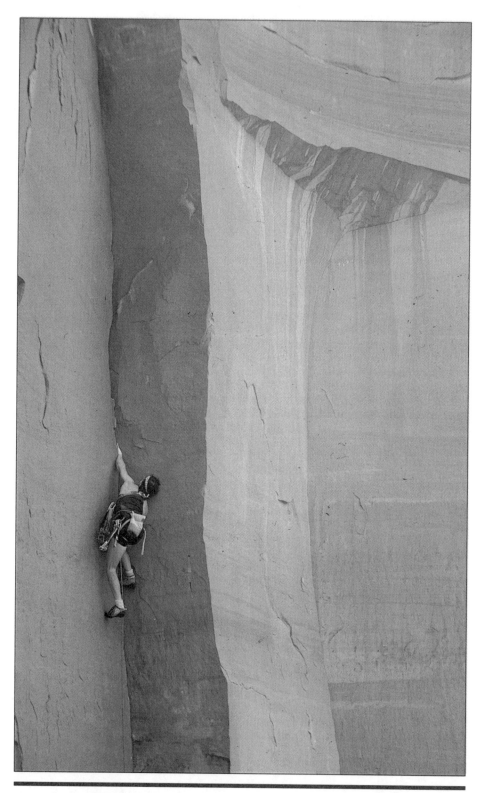

foot on it's side so your inside ankle faces up. Slot the foot in the crack, then pivot the foot toward the horizontal. As you weight it, keep trying to rotate it tighter in the crack. Properly set, such foot jams easily support the bulk of your weight. It's a mistake to think the foot jam improves the deeper you set your boot, however. Keeping the foot as far out of the crack as can be easily secured allows easy removal and keeps your center of gravity away from the rock and a bit of your weight off your arms. You rarely have to stick the boot in past the ball of the foot. Any constrictions make foot jams that much more secure. Always try and keep the feet relatively low, and the legs somewhat straight. The higher the feet, the more your rump hangs out and the more you hang on your arms.

Fist Jamming

Even experienced climbers find fist jamming a precarious technique, in part because it's seldom used, but mostly because the fist jam rarely feels quite right. The jam is set by clinching the fist, which enlarges the small muscles on the outside of the hand; and since these expand very little, the best fist jam is usually a matter of matching fist size with crack size. When the fit is snug, the fist jam is very secure.

Look for a constriction to jam above. If the crack is parallel sided, choose the spot where your fist fits snugly. Sometimes you will slot the fist straight in, like a boxer throwing a slow-motion jab. The fist is then flexed as the hand is rotated into the vertical position. Other times the fist is simply placed vertically and the hand flexed. Depending on the crack, the fist, once slotted, can assume several basic forms. With an exact fit, the thumb is wrapped across the index and middle finger. The thumb may be tucked across the palm on a tight fit. On an ultra-thin fist jam, let the middle and third finger float above the index finger and the pinky, which narrows the profile of the fist. This "ball-jam" can be expanded very little, and is only "bomber" above a constriction. (A wide hand jam is usually preferable over the "ball-jam".) An even less reliable position is sometimes (though very rarely) used when the crack is too wide. Keep the thumb on the outside of the fist, braced over, or against the index finger. This is a painful, and most often make-shift jam which will rarely bear much weight. Sometimes the flex of a forearm inserted into the crack will add security to a loose jam.

On straight-in fist cracks it is often possible to jam the entire crack with the back of the hands facing out. However, many climbers prefer to jam the lower fist palm out, finding the strain is distributed over a greater range of muscles. Picture yourself picking up a big barrel, then tilting the barrel horizontally. Your arms would form a circle, with the lower hand palm up, supporting the barrel. If your lower hand was palm down, the barrel would be resting, no doubt precariously, on the back of the hand. Turn your hand over, and you kick in the full power of your shoulder,

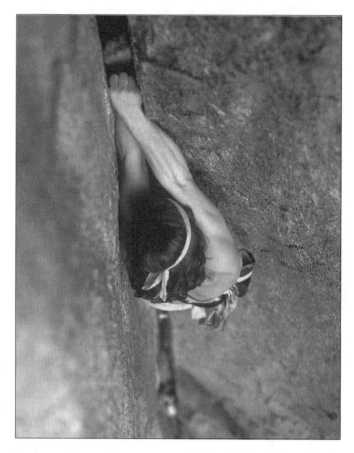

Fists torqued tight, Nic Taylor punches through "Twilight Zone" (5.10d), Yosemite Valley

George Meyers photo

back, and biceps. With extreme fist cracks, by jamming the lower fist palm-up, you form a sort of ring of power; and using this configuration, many of the hardest fist cracks have been climbed.

When the crack leans, you will invariably use this technique. Also, unlike jamming thinner cracks, you will seldom reach above the upper fist with the lower one, for this is most often too awkward. Better to shuffle the fists up the crack, locking off the lower jam, and reaching above for the next one.

Fist cracks are often very strenuous; and even world-class climbers are prone to rotate their jams. Again, dreadful abrasions can result, so many climbers opt to tape their hands for even moderate fist cracks. Check the end of this chapter for details.

Since the breadth of your hand and foot is roughly the same, if your fist fits, so will your feet. Look for a constriction. Otherwise, the foot goes straight in. If it's loose, torque it laterally for stability. As with all jamming, try and keep the feet low, and the weight over them. Resist the temptation of kicking the boot into the crack, or jamming it too deeply. The boot can get stuck, and it's no fun trying to extract it.

Off-Width Cracks

Off-width, or off-sized cracks are too wide for fist jamming and too narrow for anything but the knee, if that. The extreme off-width crack is far and away the most feared prospect in all of climbing. There is simply no easy means to climb them, and success often involves more grunting and cursing than finesse and elegance because very few climbers have taken time to master this, the most awkward technique of all. The reasons are several. Very few climbing areas have many off-width cracks, and if you can't practice, you'll never master them. The technique is more battle than dance, and in an era of spandex leggings and hot pink boots, off-width cracks are about as popular as walking barefoot in the snow. History also plays a part in the disdain climbers have for off-width stuff. In the early sixties, America's greatest climbs were in Yosemite Valley, and most featured off-width climbing. When up-and-coming climbers wanted to bag the big-name routes, they had no choice but to tackle these off-width testpieces. The first few encounters were desperate, thrashing, villainous affairs; but they stuck to it, and one season was usually enough to master the technique. As the newer generations turned towards thinner cracks, the nasty off-widths were gratefully overlooked, and today, most climbers simply avoid the technique because they lack the requisite experience for the climb to be anything but a pitched battle.

OFFWIDTH TECHNIQUE

Set the feet, one leg torqued high in the crack, perhaps heel-toeing, the other on the outside of the crack in a heel-toe. The arms, set in arm bars or locks, provide the stability for the feet to step the body up the crack.

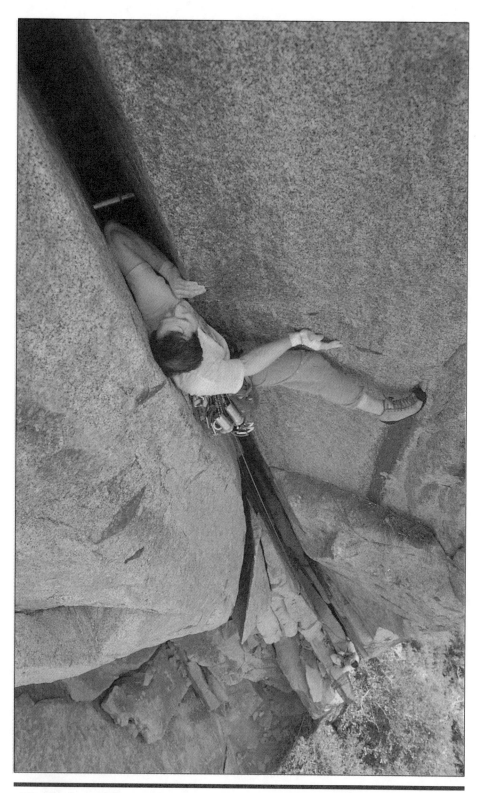

If one of the international climbing competitions were staged on an overhanging, 5.13 off-width, we'd probably see contestants trying to paw up the bald face on either side of the crack.

The most arduous off-widths are about four inches wide, where you *cannot* get your knee in. Upward progress involves locking off the upper body, moving the legs up, locking them off, then jack-knifing the upper body back up. Repeated ad nauseam, this sequence makes the Eight Labors of Hercules seem like light housework.

You must first decide whether to climb left or right-side in. In a vertical crack, if the crack is off set, you will probably climb with your back against the raised edge, which may provide a little extra leverage. If the crack edges are uniform, or flush, you find what side of the crack has the best edge and/or footholds. While the outside arm grips the outside edge, the inside arm is locked inside the crack. In thin off-size (normally 4" and 5"), the back of the upper arm is held in place by pushing the palm against the opposite side—the classic "arm-bar". The outside arm can add torque by pulling out on the crack's edge. For optimum leverage, place the arm bar diagonally down and away from the shoulder. This kicks in the front deltoid and upper chest muscles, and adds to the fulcrum effect of the arm bar. If you cannot get your knee inside the crack, you must jam your inside foot (and sometimes your calf), usually by torquing it horizontally. Make sure to use any edges or stem holds for the outside leg. Once the feet are set, the outside hand moves up and pulls hard against the lip of the crack, then the arm bar is quickly shuffled up and locked off, usually level with, or just beneath the outside hand. Then the process is repeated. If the crack is overhanging and you can't get the knee in, the hardest part is moving the arm bar up. Sometimes this is only possible with little dynamic hops, shuffling the arm bar up and quickly locking it before you fall out backwards.

Once the crack opens up enough to get a knee inside, the technique is much more manageable. While the jack-knife motion may still be necessary to move up, your lower body can now be securely jammed. The inside leg is in a vertical version of the arm-bar, with hip, thigh, knee, heel, and toe all torqued and counter pressuring. Both the outside and inside foot should be in a heel-toe jam. Keep the toes lower than the heel, which allows the toes to be smeared for better purchase. The outside leg is usually set above the inside leg, with the knee pointed up and out of the crack. If you are either very slim, flexible, or if the crack opens up enough, the arm bar can be replaced with the "arm lock", or "accordion jam". Much like the arm bar, you simply fold the forearm back and palm against the opposite side of the crack. Many times, the natural muscular tension in your arms and a little upper body English will make the arm lock so snug it's hard to even move it. Some climbers augment the arm bar with the arm lock; just as many find it too awkward and only

(page opposite)

Bruce Bailey sets an arm lock on the rugged Twilight Zone (5.10d), in Yosemite. Note the foot bridged out right and the mammoth chock slotted above his head.

John Sherman photo

use it to rest. When the crack widens too much to use the heel-toe jam, you must start foot-stacking, the most called on stack being the "T-bar".

The T-Bar

The best sequence of when to move what is a matter of what the crack dictates, and what process works best for you. Experience is the best and only teacher, but remember the following points: Resist the natural temptation of sticking your body deep into the crack. It may feel more secure, but it inhibits your mobility. So stay outside of the crack as much as possible. And don't thrash. Set each limb solidly, and keep it locked as the others shuffle up. Don't rush, pace yourself, rely on small movements rather than drastic lunging; and never skip the chance to rest. Wear sufficient clothing to protect against the inevitable scrapes. Remember that most off-widths are rated for people who know exactly what they are doing. As a beginner you may find even a moderate off-width climb the hardest thing you've ever done. After you have a few under your harness, go back and see what a huge difference experience and technique make.

Hand Stacking

Also known as "Leavittation" (after a pioneer of this technique), this technique supplants the strenuous arm bar with a variety of two-handed jamming configurations: Fist against hand, hand against hand, fist against fist. This technique should work anywhere that hands can be stacked, and the lower body can at least momentarily support the whole body

via knee jams and/or calf locks. Leavittation is particularly efficient on straight-in, off-width cracks so desperate or overhanging that pure arm barring is prohibitive, if not impossible. Only practice can show you what kinds of hand stacks work—there are no rules or "best jam" guidelines. It's the jammed legs that are the real trick.

The basic sequence is: Find a hand stack, then a knee lock as high as possible below the hand stack. This "active" leg is soon to bear your full bulk, so work it in as securely as possible. The "passive" leg is heel and toe jamming below, and is mainly a balance point. You must then release the hand stack and establish another above, the high knee-jam supporting your weight, while your abdominals keep you upright. Then repeat the process.

The knee lock is key, tough to master, and is usually where even experienced climbers fail with leavittation. The secret is to keep it as high as possible. For optimum torque, once the knee is completely inside the crack, bend it back so it locks and allows you to bring your foot back out of the crack. The foot is in turn placed against the outside of the crack, supplying a sort of brace effect that allows you to let go with both hands and set up the next hand stack.

A straight-in crack allows a choice for the "active" or jammed knee; the leaning crack does not. If the crack leans right, jam the left knee; if left, jam the right one. Leavittation is a very advanced technique that takes practice to even understand. It's normal application is on off-width cracks at the very top of the scale and of a fairly narrow range of size.

Flares, and Squeeze Chimneys

By definition, any crack too wide to heel-toe jam but only wide enough to barely accept the body is a squeeze chimney. They may be easy to slide into, but usually they are strenuous and almost claustrophobic to ascend. A bottoming, or shallow squeeze chimney is a flare. Once it is too wide to use an arm lock or accordion jam with the arms, it's a chimney. These techniques often overlap on a given climb, but we'll look at them separately to focus on the various methods of climbing them.

Squeeze chimneys are climbed using off-width techniques with a few additional tricks and variations. The arm lock is the stand-by for the arms, though a wide arm bar, and even an inverted arm bar (elbow higher than the palm) is often used. You can typically get inside a squeeze chimney, so the arm lock and arm bar variants can be used with both arms. The normal configuration sees the arm lock for the inside arm, and the inverted arm bar for the outside arm. Sometimes, both arms are using the inverted arm bar.

Foot stacking, the T-bar should be used if at all possible. If the chimney is too wide, press both knees against the front wall, with both feet torqued flat against the back wall. The opposing pressures between knees and feet keep the lower body in place. Like off-width cracks, the lower and upper body move up alternatively.

Many squeeze chimneys are so slim you have to exhale to move up. Most chimneys narrow the farther you enter them, so fight the urge to work deeper—albeit more securely—into the bowels of the crack and stay toward the outside, where movement is easier. You'll probably find that staying lodged is easy, but moving up is difficult. Just climb slowly, work it out, and never get frantic.

Flares are wide enough to get inside, but too shallow to do so very far. They can be nasty undertakings, very strenuous and insecure, and technical riddles. Because every flare is a little different, they defy much generic explanation. Still, almost every flare requires the inside arm to be arm locking; and often the purchase of elbow and palm is marginal. The outside hand will exploit any hand hold, ar at least vigorously palm off the flare to augment the arm lock. The feet are bridging—inside foot back-stepping the back wall, outside foot pressing off any footholds available—or, simply frictioning, flat against the face. Sometimes you alternate these

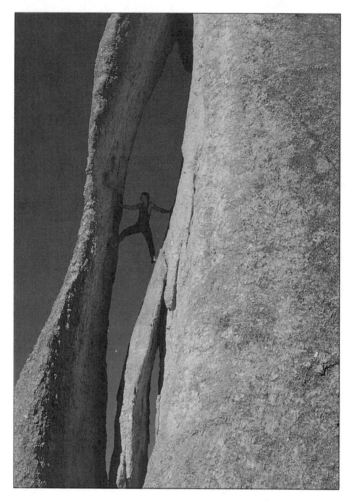

The way is straight, the gate narrow. Robert Finlay bridges up through the "Needle's Eye" (5.8) in the Black Hills of South Dakota. At this juncture, the chimney is moderate and wide enough to march a camel through, but ten feet overhead, the slot narrows and only the chosen can toil on.

Bob Gaines photo

tasks between outside and inside feet. The outside foot is key, for it presses the buttocks and back against the back wall; so the decision which way to face often depends on where the footholds are. Many times you won't know which way to face until you try. If the flare is extremely shallow, very steep, and devoid of footholds, you're looking at a nasty piece of work, where anything goes.

Chimneys

When cracks widen enough so that they are easily entered, they may lose some degree of security, but they are usually much easier to climb. Knee chimneys are just that. Bridging is done between knees and back, variations in size being accomodated by flaring the knees to varying degrees. Movement is a ratcheting affair, with the arm usually in the inverted arm bar position. Knee chimneys are usually secure. Knee pads can prevent painful bruises to the knee caps and a long sleeved shirt will protect the shoulders.

When the chimney is wider than the distance between your knee and your foot, you push the feet against one wall and the back against the other. To move up, one foot backsteps off the back wall so your legs form a bridge via opposing pressures. The hands are either pressing off the far wall or are bridged between both walls, like the feet. In either case, the back is released and the legs extended; the torso moves up and the back is again pressed against the back wall. Opposing pressures between hands and back allow the feet to either shuffle up or to exchange positions—front foot now backstepping, back foot now pressing off the far wall. Always let the legs do the pushing. Foot-back chimneys should never be strenuous for the arms.

If the chimney is wider than the distance between your hips and feet, you can "bridge" it, using one hand and one foot on each wall, each limb pressing directly out. If your purchase is attained by pure friction, this is rough duty, so keep an eye peeled for any footholds or shelves to bridge off.

In chimneys too big to bridge, it is theoretically possible to lodge yourself dead horizontal, facing straight down, with both feet on one wall, and both hands on the other—like a clothes rack in a closet. Most expert climbers have done this for a couple of moves somewhere. I've heard climbers claim

Knee chimney

Foot-back chimney

they had done this on long routes, up vertical shafts for hundreds of feet, and I don't believe a word of it. I can't imagine not falling if you had to do the "clothes rack" for more than a few feet. Don't believe everything you hear. And if something sounds absurd, it probably is.

Liebacking

"Hanging on for dear life" is often the description given for the full-blown, all-out lieback. Fortunately, few liebacks are all-out, but most are athletic and strenuous. Liebacking is perhaps the most exhilarating technique (outside of dynamics) in the climbing game. You can span amazing sections of rock. It's also the quickest way to find hell in a handbasket for, owing to the great opposing pressures, if your hands fail, you fire off like you're spring-loaded. In it's pure form, the technique is used to climb aretes, cracks in right-angled corners, or cracks which are too shallow for jamming. In it's partial form, any time you lean off a hold you are liebacking, for you are lying back off the face hold, the jug, the edge of the crack, or whatever your hands are on. It's a means to use holds that are other than simple horizontal edges.

The lieback

The basic motion is: pulling with your hands, pushing with your feet, one in opposition to the other. A typical lieback will find your side flush against the wall. Your hands are clasping the near edge of the crack, and you are liebacking off them. Your feet are pressing against the crack's far edge, are balanced on small holds, are vigorously pushing off a corner's far wall, or maybe are even jammed in the crack. There are many quasi forms of liebacking, but all involve the upper torso leaning off to one side and your arms pulling toward yourself.

The purest and most typical lieback occurs on a flake leaning against the wall or in a crack in a 90-degree corner—a dihedral.

Your hands are pulling directly out, and your feet are pushing the opposite way, directly against the face or far wall. Since the technique is strenuous, try and keep the arms straight, which, again, lets the skeletal system, rather than the muscles, absorb at least some of the strain. Many times it is possible and desirable to leap frog the hands, one over the other; but often the top hand will remain on top throughout, shuffling the lower hand up to it, then reaching above with that top hand. On steep liebacks, you'll never want the hands to loose contact with the liebacked edge, so the hands are slid up, perhaps even under pressure. Also, leap-frogging your limbs can sometimes get you crossed up, throwing your body out of balance. Try and keep your feet as low as possi-

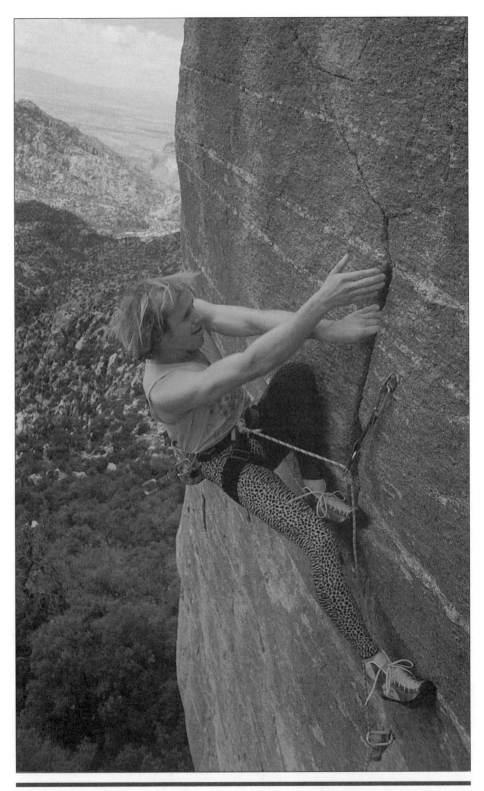

ble, using any footholds. The closer your feet are to your hands, the more strenuous the lieback becomes.

The full-blown or "Frankenstein" lieback is most often found in a steep or overhanging corner. The crack's edge might be rounded or the crack so thin it will accept only fingertips. The opposite wall may be overhung, slanting away and smooth as glass, so your feet gain purchase only through the friction of direct pressure. The "Frankenstein" lieback entails drawing your feet up by your hands and "swinging" into the all-out, liebacking posture. The problem is, not only is this extremely strenuous, but there's often the tendency to swing right out, like a door opening on it's hinges. This "barndoor" effect can be countered either by increasing the torque to both hands and feet (which makes things more strenuous still), or by bridging the outside foot out and pushing obliquely off the far wall, hoping to stall the swing and regain equilibrium. Sometimes you must momentarily palm off the opposite wall to halt the swing. Sometimes it is possible to jam the inside foot in the crack, keeping the other foot stemmed out wide to provide a hinge-proof base. If you're fortunate, the opposite wall will be peppered with big footholds. If not, it's Frankenstein all the way.

Most liebacks require a clever mix of all these techniques, though when to use what is fairly intuitive once you've swung into the lieback. Your body responds automatically to changes in equilibrium and variations in angle but always try and keep the arms straight. Feel the edge of the lieback as much as possible, and crank off the sharpest, most defined spots. Look for any stem or rest holds, but don't stop if it's more strenuous than carrying on. Climb aggressively, and don't hang about looking for footholds which aren't readily apparent. The exhortation, "go for it!", was invented for the climber swinging into a lieback. Once committed, don't hesitate: power over it quickly.

Stemming

(page opposite)

Stem, Jim! Jim Waugh splays up "Bachs Celebration" (5.12a), at Paradise Forks, Arizona. This three-sided slot is utterly bereft of holds, so full-blown stemming— ratcheting each limb up in turn—is Jim's only hope to celebrate.

Bill Hatcher photo

Stemming, or "bridging", normally occurs in right-angled corners, where the crack is non-existent or so thin as to be of little value. Many times it is necessary when the crack momentarily pinches down. Even when the crack is good, your lower body may stem the whole way. In any case, stemming is essentially face climbing in a corner.

Many difficult climbs involve stemming, and the extreme stemming problem can require creative sequences and very improbable, marginal counter pressures. Consider the stemming corner as an ultra-flared chimney. In it's pure form, the feet are pasted on opposite walls, perhaps frictioning, maybe smearing on footholds, but counter pressuring against themselves and/or the hands. The hands may also be cross pressuring, palming off the slightest irregularities, or pawing holds. Essentially, your body is like a spring lodged between two sloping walls. The only thing keeping the spring in place

is the purchase at both ends, and the tension between. Moving the spring up, then, is the hard part, for this requires the tension to go lax, at least momentarily, yet it never can. Usually it's the diagonal pressure of one hand and one foot that keeps the climber in place, and the climber alternates this bridge in moving up. This can involve a dozen little moves to gain even a foot of upward progress. Sometimes you may actually chimney the corner, back against one wall, feet smearing off the other. You may back step with one boot, edge with the other, palm with one hand, and mantle with the other. The possibilities are endless. Flexibility, balance and the ability to exploit any and all features are a stemmer's tools.

Protecting With Tape

Perfect technique does not eliminate painful hand abrasions altogether. Some cracks are lined with crystals, others require awkward, shallow jamming, notorious for shredding even expert hands; and overhanging fist cracks are almost always good for a few "gobis". A popular solution is taping. There are dozens of taping patterns, none so good to preclude all others (one is illustrated at left), but certain tips apply to all taping methods.

First, remove hair from your hands and wrists (and the palms, too, should you have any there). Shaving will work, but singing the hair off with a low level flame is even better. The tape will adhere well only if you apply a chemical taping base, such as tincture of benzoin or Cramer's Tuf-skin, both available at sporting goods stores. Apply the taping base only where the tape will go, otherwise the bald areas will collect dirt and the skin will feel greasy. Also, don't use waterproof tape, only cloth or "coaches tape" (commonly available in one and a half-inch width). Following the procedure outlined in the photos, start with half-width strips, pinched at the center, that loop the base of the fingers. Next, bind these to the wrist. Finally, should extra reinforcement be necessary, apply selected lateral strips to tie the finger strips together. As you tape, flex the hand and wrist to stretch the skin, otherwise the tape will limit hand expansion and decrease jamming force. Tape loosely, especially around the wrist. Tight taping cuts circulation and hinders flexibility. Should you already have some "gobis", place a small piece of tape upside down over the abrasion to avoid ripping the scab off when you remove the tape.

We have reviewed the salient points of physically climbing rock. The psychology and strategy of putting it all together, in conjunction with the process of safe rope management, can be done only after we have a working knowledge of equipment.

Ropes, Anchors, and Belays: The Protection System

No climber ever gets very good without falling, and the falling climber is quickly killed without a solid, dependable protection system. The protection system combines bombproof anchors, ropes, connecting links, and alert partners to provide a sort of safety net which keeps him from hitting the ground. When you see a climber lashed to the cliff, all the odd-looking widgits and knots and whatnot can look complicated. Actually, the system is quite simple once you understand what the gear is and how it all works.

We see the climber moving up the dark cliff, secured by a rope and partner above. Who got that line up there? Somebody had to go first, and had he fallen, he would have died a horrible death—right? Wrong. The whole point of the rope and the attending gear, along with the hundred years that went into refining both technique and equipment, is to safeguard the climbers in the event of a fall. Sport climbing is not the pastime of nihilists or madmen; and when a world-class climber starts an extreme climb, he knows he will fall dozens, even hundreds of times. And he doesn't expect to get hurt. When the beginner starts up his first climb, the aim should be to have fun, not to cheat death.

In a nutshell: two climbers are tied into their respective ends of a 150- or 165-foot rope. Starting from the ground, one climber secures himself ("anchors") off to a tree, a big block, or perhaps arranges an anchor with some of his specialized gear fitted into a handy crack. In any case, his anchor is not what it should be unless it is *failsafe*. Having decided on a particular passage, or "route" up the cliff—say a prominent crack—the other climber (the "leader") starts up, scaling the crack using hands and feet. The man on the ground (the "belayer") is meanwhile paying out the rope, using a technique or mechanical device which can stop the rope cold if need be.

Now the leader has gained a difficult section. He removes an appropriate piece of gear from his sling, places it in the crack, tugs it to get a good seating, clips a carabiner (snaplink) through the gear, then clips his rope through the carabiner. The leader now has an anchor which "protects" him for the climbing just overhead. Say he climbs three feet above the anchor and falls. The belayer checks the rope; the leader falls twice the distance he is above the anchor, or six feet. Since the rope stretches, he might fall inches more, but the belayer, lashed to his anchor and holding the fall, doesn't budge. The leader gathers his wits, and tries again.

A question. If the leader was only three feet above the anchor, why did he fall six feet plus the odd extra inches? First, for several reasons, the belayer cannot effectively take in the rope when the leader falls. His duty is to lock the rope off, so when the leader's weight comes onto the rope, the rope is held fast. If the leader is three feet above his anchor—or "protection"—he must first fall three feet *to* that protection. He still has three feet of slack out, so he falls *three more feet,* past the protection, for a total fall of six feet plus, depending on rope stretch. Hence the equation: The leader falls twice the distance above his last protection—and then some.

Carrying on, the leader places protection as he sees fit, always placing something before a hard section. Sixty feet up the crack, he might have placed six or eight pieces of protection, depending on the difficulty and how secure he feels. Once the leader gains a convenient place to stop—say a ledge or a stout tree—he in turn arranges an anchor which is *absolutely failsafe.* In this case, that means an anchor strong enough that, no matter what the other climber does, no matter how far he falls, he cannot cause the anchor to fail or come out. Now it is the leader's turn to "belay", or to take the rope in as the "second" follows the "pitch", or rope length. As the second follows, he removes all the protection which the leader placed, so it may be used on the next pitch. Since the belayer is taking up the rope as the second climbs up to him, the second can only fall as far as the rope stretches, usually only a foot or so, and mere inches if little rope is out. Once the second reaches the leader's anchor, or "belay", he in turn takes over the lead while the erstwhile leader continues belaying and the process is repeated until the team finishes the route.

This is free climbing; note that the gear is not used for upward progress. The leader does not hang from the gear he places, rather he climbs using only hands and feet. In free climbing, the gear is used *only to safeguard against a fall.* The sport is to climb the rock using your own physical abilities. Rope and gear are what make the process sane and allow you to push your limits, saving your life should you fall off. Since falling has become an integral part of sport climbing, both the system and the gear are very reliable but, once again, it's all in how you use them and the most fundamental item, the rope, is no good if you're not on it or it's not anchored.

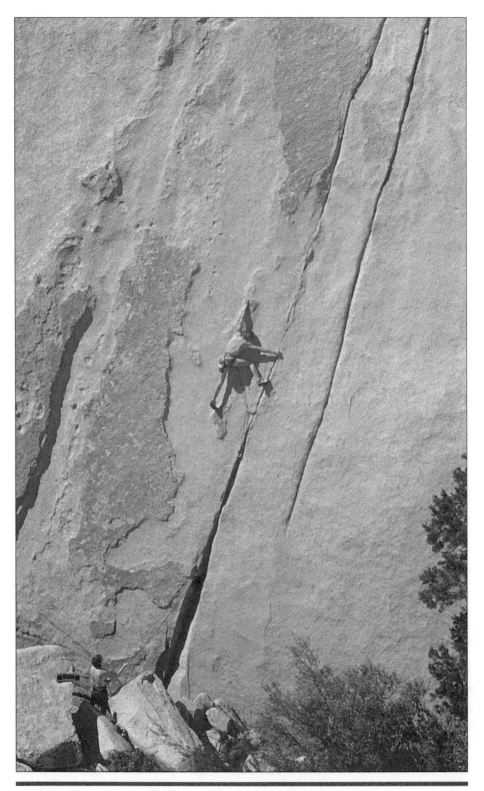

The rope is your lifeline, the primary piece of equipment to any climber. There is not a single serious climber whose life has not been saved by the rope, so obviously modern climbing ropes are extremely reliable. Modern ropes have evolved a long way from the horsehair cords of the Carthaginians and from the dicey hemp lines the pioneers used around Zermatt and other alpine villages, where accounts of ropes snapping were many and tragic. Those early hemp ropes were replaced, first by flax, then with cotton varieties from European-grown fibers. Phillipines "manila" and sisal from Mexico in turn succeeded these, and by World War II, a dense, three-strand "balloon" manila and a similar four-strand yachting rope (white line) were the only choices for an alpinist. During the war, Arnold Wexler of the U.S. Bureau of Standards concluded that for strength, elasticity, and durability, nylon was superior to all natural blends. Since 1945, all viable climbing ropes have been fashioned from nylon, or "perlon", a continental trade-name for a plastic similar to nylon.

Though there are isolated cases of ropes being cut over sharp edges or chopped by rock fall, *a modern climbing rope has never simply broken from the impact of a fall.* Not in the United States, not in Europe; not anywhere. There is so much overkill built into the system that a rope in good condition has *no* chance of breaking whatsoever, no matter how severe a fall you take on it.

All modern climbing ropes are "kernmantle" ("jacketed-core"), comprised of a woven nylon sheath over a braided core. Prior to 1970, one viable alternative to kernmantle was

"goldline", a nylon rope of "twisted", or "Hawser-laid" construction, where three or four main strands were twisted around each other. Though goldline handled poorly and stretched like a rubber band, it was plenty strong, and at half the price of kernmantle it was popular. For several reasons, goldline became a forgotten commodity and, though many of America's most noted climbs were accomplished on goldline, I haven't seen anyone climbing on one in fifteen years.

The standard dimensions of a modern climbing rope are 50 meters (165 feet) in length, and 10, 10.5, or 11 millimeters in diameter. There are 8 and 9 millimeter ropes which have specific applications we will discuss in later chapters.

Kernmantle rope

For decades, a 150-foot length rope was the standard. You can still purchase one of this length, but there are more and more situations where a climb has been engineered to require a 165-foot rope and, should you not have one when you need it, you will be cussing yourself for the few dollars saved in buying the shorter line.

Experts have conducted exhaustive studies on the various qualities of kernmantle ropes and have presented complicated graphs and formulas that seem impossible to understand. All the rare terminology and physics actually pertains to basic concepts, easily understood if simply explained. It all starts with the Union Internationale des Associations D'Alpinisme—UIAA—an international organization which sets minimum standards that commercially available rope should meet. Rope manufacturers provide both the UIAA findings and anything else they have been able to independently prove which might give them a marketing edge, but there are only a few specifications which relate directly to performance. The first relates to the number of falls sustained before the rope breaks in a UIAA-simulated drop test.

In this drop test, they tie an 80 kg iron block to the end of a 2.8 meter length of rope. They secure the other end to a fixed anchor, using .3 meters for the anchoring set up. They then raise the iron block 2.5 meters above the anchor point and drop it for a total free-fall of 5 meters. Common sense would tell us that a far longer fall would better gauge a rope's strength, but this is untrue. Kernmantle ropes have fantastic dynamic qualities, meaning they stretch when fallen on. Consequently, the longer the fall, the more rope there is out to absorb the dynamic energy generated by a falling climber. So it's these short falls, where the rope stretches comparatively little, that most stress the rope. Experts all agree that, for various reasons, the UIAA test is more severe than any fall you could possibly take in the field. Indeed, the UIAA simulated fall is so severe that it's about like tying off a dairy cow and marching her off the cliff's edge for a 300-footer. Yet a rope must withstand five UIAA test drops to be approved. Various manufacturers have gone on to make ropes they claim can withstand up to 13 test falls, but since the UIAA approval means a rope is stronger than you'll ever need, the 13 fall figure is altogether meaningless. The original kernmantle ropes were approved if they held only two UIAA drops yet, in actual practice, none of these ropes ever broke. So if a two-fall rope never broke, why would you need a 13 fall rope? You don't. If a rope is UIAA approved, it will never break in the field. The rest is sophistry.

The next spec is weight, which would be an important consideration if ropes of the same dimension differed much. Of the six leading rope manufacturers, the lightest 11 millimeter rope is 72 grams per meter, the heaviest, 79 grams per meter; so weight is a negligible factor.

"Static" or "working elongation" basically refers to how much a rope stretches when weighted with an 80 kg iron block. The leading ropes vary little here. "Impact force elongation"—how far the rope stretches when fallen on—is far more important, but is seldom listed in the statistics, probably because it requires very sophisticated equipment to measure this. I.F.E. is a real consideration, since the longer a rope stretches, the farther you fall, which increases the likelihood of hitting something. The available specs from most leading manufacturers vary from about 6 to 7 percent I.F.E. Negligible, you say? Maybe, but the difference might be six inches in a 40-foot fall; and as rope physicist Dennis Turvill has pointed out, "a fall six inches longer can mean the difference between a good bar story and a compound fracture." Hopefully, impact force elongation will soon become a required statistic for all ropes.

"Impact force" pertains to the degree of shock the body receives at the end of a fall. This is crucial, since a greater force means a more jarring, painful stop. Different brands can vary as much as 10 percent, so some thought should be directed to this statistic.

Another factor is whether or not a rope has been treated with a waterproofing compound. Compounds differ amongst manufacturers. Some are paraffin-based and come off the rope quickly. The better coatings are of silicone and various fluorochemicals, the latter being the best for durability. Though nothing can keep a rope dry in a deluge, tests prove that coated ropes are 33 percent more abrasion resistant than uncoated ropes. Also, coating greatly reduces the ability of the rope to absorb damaging U.V. rays; and for these two reasons, coatings do more for a rope's longevity than the number of falls they allegedly hold.

Different sheath characteristics—the tightness of the weave, and whether the sheath slips much—directly affect how a rope handles. Ropes prone to excessive kinking, which are stiff and hold knots poorly, and which get twisted and spin a suspended climber, are really dastardly things to use. Unfortunately, it is difficult to determine a rope's handling characteristics when it is brand new, and there is little objective information which honestly pegs these qualities. Moreover, a rope which in the retail shop handles like silk might prove to be a "corkscrew" once you have used it. The sheath might shift a lot, or it may stiffen after only moderate use. Ultimately, a climber is left to review the available literature and experiment with other ropes, drawing conclusions accordingly.

Since any UIAA-approved rope is stronger than you'll ever need, most climbers tend to buy the cheapest UIAA-approved rope they can

Caring for your rope

Never step on the rope. Debris can work through the sheath to cut and abrade the core. Stepping on someone's rope is an extreme breach of decorum.

Never lend your rope to anyone. Never buy a used rope. They don't fetch much money, and there's probably a good reason why someone wants to deal it. It may have been used to tow a back-hoe out of a snow drift.

Protect your rope from unnecessary exposure to the sun; save for huge falls that result in sheath damage and careless abuse, U.V. rays are the single most destructive force your rope is exposed to, so the more time spent in sunlight, the faster it will deteriorate. Always store your rope in a cool, dry, shady place.

Contrary to common opinion, alcohol, gasoline and other hydrocarbon solvents do not affect nylon chemically; and though you should avoid exposing your rope to any foreign substance, a little gasoline is not disastrous to your rope. Battery acid and other corrosives spell instant death to your line, however.

A certain amount of grime is unavoidable. When the rope becomes obviously dirty, machine wash it in cold or warm water and mild soap. Use the delicate fabric setting and rinse it for two cycles. Avoid the dryer. Instead, string it up in a shady place, or flake it out on a clean floor and let the water evaporate naturally, normally accomplished in a couple of days.

Periodically inspect the rope for frays and soft spots by folding the rope carefully between your fingers and working it from one end to the other.

find, since the majority of climbers don't understand the implications of all the attending statistics. The ideal rope would stretch little when weighted, would have a low impact force, would handle like a mink's pelt, would weigh one pound, and would cost around five dollars. No one rope has all these characteristics, and the average price is around 130 dollars.

Despite the astronomical tensile strength of kernmantle ropes, they are made of supple nylon, which is easily damaged when even slightly abused. Since you're hanging your all on the rope, you'll want to pay extremely close attention to the use and care of your lifeline.

Chris Gore, technical consultant for Beal ropes, has laid down the following guidelines for a rope's life expectancy: "A rope should be retired after four years, even if it's used only on holidays. For normal, week-end use: two years. For multi-fall use: three months of constant use or up to a year of part-time use. Any rope suffering a long fall of great severity should be retired immediately". While not definitive, this is certainly sound advice.

A rope bag is an inexpensive and very practical way of storing your rope. There's a lot of garbage rattling around the normal pack, car, or house, and the rope bag protects your cord from these until the moment you start climbing; and the rope is re-bagged once you're done. Some climbers use them to store the slack *during* a climb, but most will find this a bit much. In extreme instances—say, climbing just above a working sea—a rope fed out of a rope bag is a saving grace.

WEBBING

Originally used to batten down gear on P.T. boats during World War II, nylon webbing (flat rope, or "tape") is an integral part of a climber's equipment. When tied into a loop (forming a "runner", or "sling") its applications range from gear slings and extensions for anchors, to make-shift harnesses, all to be further explained. For now, understand that for fifth class climbing, webbing comes in four widths: 2, 1, $\frac{11}{16}$, and $\frac{9}{16}$ inch. This webbing is often times tubular—hollow inside—and is incredibly strong.

The most common use for webbing is for runners. These are tied in single loops made from about four to six feet of 1, $\frac{5}{8}$, or $\frac{9}{16}$ inch webbing, and are carried over one shoulder and under the opposite arm. The length will vary according to your size. The runner should never be so long that, when carried, the bottom hangs below your waist, where it can easily snag on the rock, or even on your foot during a high step. Runners are used somewhere on virtually every climb, and it is a common error not to have enough. Some sources advise you to carry upwards of a dozen, but such advice invariably comes from those hawking climbing gear. Most climbers find five or six runners more than adequate for all but exceptional cases.

The Ring Bend

Double Fisherman's

Sewn slings and runners are becoming increasingly popular. The pre-sewn joints dispense with the knot, which is sometimes a hindrance. Their disadvantage is that they cannot be untied and connected with other slings to form a king-sized runner should the need arise, as it will.

Be cautious when using any sewn gear. In their original state the stitching is stronger than the webbing. However, the stitching abrades with use, and the overall strength is significantly reduced. It is a good practice to inspect any sewn webbing periodically. Most climbers carry a collection of both sewn and tied slings.

Webbing is generally sound until, from exposure to U.V. and general wear, it becomes stiff to the touch. If there's any doubt, pitch them. Though it's exceptionally rare, old slings have broken. And never use a sling you have found or fleeced off the crag. A sling is usually left because someone "bailed", decided to retreat. The runner was secured to an anchor, the rope doubled through the runner, and down they went. To retrieve the rope, they had to pull it through the sling; and pulling even 50 feet of rope through a sling can generate sufficient friction and heat to greatly diminish the strength of the webbing by melting the nylon. Visual inspection can tell you much—faded color or notible stiffness, for instance—but not all. Some climbers like to date their slings with a felt pen, and pitch them after one year's use. Remember to treat your slings with the respect due your rope.

A RING BEND or WATER KNOT has been the traditional knot to tie runners together. However, nylon webbing is slippery, particularly when new, and it's not unheard of for the ring bend to loosen with time and come untied. A good practice with any gear is to routinely check your knots, especially the ring bend. A much more secure albeit permanent knot for both rope and webbing is the DOUBLE FISHERMAN'S, or GRAPEVINE knot. Though it is possible to untie this knot, it becomes increasingly more arduous as the runner is weighted and stressed. Since the grapevine knot is a "cinch" knot—meaning the tighter you pull, the tighter it gets—just a few climbs is usually enough to make this knot more or less impossible to untie. Should any knot prove difficult to untie, some gentle taps with a smooth rock will often loosen it enough to get the fingers in. There will be more on runners in the chapter: The Art of Leading.

CONNECTING THE CLIMBER TO THE ROPE

The bowline is the most basic and therefore the first knot a climber should learn in order to tie into the rope. For decades this was the accepted way to tie in. The main disadvantage with the bowline is that it's very uncomfortable when weighted, tending to cut into a climber's side or work up the rib cage when fallen on. The bowline-on-a-coil is a more comfortable variation of the bowline that is worthwhile to know. Disadvantages: the knot uses a lot of rope, a hinderance on long pitches, and, like the bowline, the bowline-on-a-

The Bowline-on-a-coil. Finish up with a half-hitch check knot as illustrated above.

coil cannot, by definition, be used should there be need to rappel or anchor to the cliff independent of the rope. Since the advent of tubular webbing, and the invention of the swami belt and harnesses, the bowline-on-a-coil has fallen out of favor. Still, it is absolutely secure and works dependably in a pinch.

Swami-Belt

A swami-belt provides a secure means for the climber to remain anchored without using the rope. It consists of four or five turns of wide webbing around the waist, secured with a ring bend. The wraps should be snug but not constricting. It takes some practice to tie the ring bend, still keeping the swami snug. A loose swami-belt is hazardous as it can creep up one's torso, inhibiting breathing and crimping the ribcage. The basic swami was originally constructed from 1-inch webbing, but as soon as 2-inch webbing was available, everyone switched over to the wider, stronger, and more comfortable webbing. Tie the ring bend with a generous tail—plenty of extra webbing beyond the knot. Once tied, slide the knot around your back, occasionally inspecting it for peace of mind. Falling on a swami or simple rope tie-in is not as uncomfortable as it may sound; with the tightening rope the swami pulls up snugly underneath the rib cage. Hanging for very long on a simple swami is distinctly uncomfortable—even dangerous, however, and most climbers will prefer the comfort and safety of either leg loops or a sewn harness.

Leg Loops

Leg loops are made of usually broad webbing, sewn into channels for each leg and connected in front by a bridge sling, short, and sewn to each channel. In the back, a keeper sling feeds off one leg, goes up and over the swami, and clips into the other leg, keeping the loops from drooping in back. The tie-in passes through both the swami and the bridge sling on the loops. The tie-in knot should be snug to both.

Leg loops and webbing swami belt

The benefit of leg loops is that whenever you put your weight on the equipment—and the times are many—that weight is taken principally on the legs rather than the back. The varieties of leg loops available are countless: Padded, fleece-lined, day-glo colors, some even faced with sham animal hide. But in actual design, they are all fundamentally the same. Make certain they fit correctly: snug, but not constricting when the legs are fully flexed. Put them on and do a few deep knee bends. If they bind the thighs, too tight; if they droop, too loose. Reputable brands are made in sizes from extra small to extra large. One size is bound to fit you perfectly.

When used in conjunction with a two-inch swami you enjoy the strongest tie-in system possible, at least twice as strong as any other link in the climbing chain, including the rope.

Harnesses

A harness features a waist strap and leg loops that are sewn into one unit. The harness has come into it's own only recently. Though they've been around for 20 years, they were of such questionable quality that a popular instruction manual published less than ten years ago barely mentioned them. The first batch were cumbersome, uncomfortable, shoddily made, and put withering constriction on genitalia during a fall. Others tended to leave one hanging sideways, even upside down after a fall. Present day har-

nesses are featherweight, stronger than neces-sary, and fit so well it's hard to remember you even have one on. There are hundreds to choose from, and with a little shopping it's easy to find the right one. Most manufacturers make several models—for mountain climbing, sixth class climbing, and general sport climb-ing; it is the latter style that are often the light-est and most comfortable.

A good harness should be easy to put on. During all around use, it should be comfort-able and not feature unnecessary buckles, joints, or any pressure points which can abrade the climber like a burr under the saddle. A good fit is critical to the performance of a har-ness, but is often impossible if your physique is

Sewn harness

even a little off the norm. You might have to try on several to get the right one. A harness is a very personal, specialized piece of gear, so general craftsmanship should reflect this. If possible, avoid adjustable harnesses which are often over-built and feature superfluous buckles and do-dads. Many harnesses have individual methods of threading the rope

through them for the best tie-in. Likewise, most harnesses have some safety procedure which, if neglected, render the harness poten-tially dangerous—a double pass-through buck-le, for example. Read any instructions careful-ly, and follow them to the letter.

Despite the thousands of woman climbers, harnesses are still built for men. Much to the manufacturers' discredit, differences in physi-cal makeup are not accounted for, and many

Many harnesses require some special buckling procedure in order for them to be secure, per-haps similar to the dou-ble pass through illustrat-ed here.

women cannot find a harness that fits well, or even poorly. A leading female climber pegged the problems: The ratio of waist to hip measurement remains fairly constant with men—not so with women. If their hips fit, the waist is too big. Most women drawn to climbing tend to be athletic, so their glutes are more muscular than non-athletic women or men of the same weight. This further complicates the fit.

But it's the disparity between hip and waist measurement that makes harnesses ill-fitting for most women. Obviously, it's time for a women's harness, so expect to see one marketed soon.

Both for women and men who cannot attain a perfect fit: Several manufacturers sell "harnesses" which are actually sewn swami belts and leg loops, sold separately. By buying a component-based combination, you can usually find a perfect fit.

The standard tie-in: the figure-eight follow-through. Be sure to loop the rope around both the waist belt or swami and the sling that bridges between the leg loops.

There is another problem which may well defy a solution. Given the morning coffee, the ready canteen, the hiking and exertion, even the world class climber will at sometime yearn for bladder relief; and neither the brash nor the bashful find any glory in just "holding it". This presents little problem for your harnessed male. Most harnesses are pretty free up front—aside from the tie-in knot—and a male's plumbing is readily deployed and can normally negotiate these obstacles, even on a wall. For women, though, the problem is real, perhaps insuperable without further technological advances.

One other type of harness bears mentioning, but in almost twenty years of climbing I have never seen someone use a chest harness, in either sport climbing or on rescue work. In sport climbing, their applications are few, if any, but there's no harm done if you have surplus cash and want to experiment with one. Supposedly, they are useful on exceptionally overhanging artificial routes, where one spends hours, or days, dangling upside down. Chest harnesses have generally been avoided, first because they are needless, and second, upper body mobility is crucial on difficult free climbs.

There are probably a dozen knots suitable for connecting the end of the rope to the swami or harness, but over the years, the figure-eight follow-through (Flemish Bend, or double figure-eight) has become standard. Like the majority of knots used in climbing (there are only about six), the figure-eight follow-through is a "cinch" knot: The tighter you pull, the tighter the knot becomes.

CARABINERS

Also known as biners (bean-ers) or krabs, a carabiner is an aluminum alloy snap-link used to connect various pieces of the climbing chain. They come in two basic designs: the oval and the D. The D has the advantage of greater strength, opens easier when weighted (important in artificial climbing), and the rope flows easier through them. Always position any D carabiner so the gate opens down and away from the rock. That way, the rope feeds through the bigger end. The oval doesn't have to be flipped over. Most climbers carry an assortment of both D's and ovals. Several other designs have slight advantages in specialized circumstances, but the basic design is the same.

Each biner features a spring-loaded gate which opens inward, accepting rope or runner, and which snaps closed when the pressure is released from the gate. All carabiners are designed to be weighted along the major axis—length-

Carabiners (clockwise from the left): oval, D, modified D, bent gate, locking type wise—and in this manner, they are exceptionally strong, some with upwards of 5,000 pounds breaking strength. (The strength of carabiners is usually marked somewhere on the gate, generally in kilograms) Under *no* circumstances should the biner ever be set up so there is pressure pulling straight out on the gate, as the biner is then only as strong as the pin upon which the gate rotates—usually under 500 pounds.

Until the climbing explosion in the mid-seventies, it was easy to find poorly-machined biners in climbing stores, and one had to use discretion in buying anything but the name-brand carabiners. Commercial competition is now so fierce that a shoddy biner has little chance of making it to the shelves, but inspect before buying just the same. The gate should have fluid action, should pivot strongly on the axis pin, and should mesh perfectly with the mouth of the biner. The finish should be smooth and burr free. And the strength should be at least 2,500 pounds (1136 kilograms).

Locking carabiner

Though durable, biners do wear out. Whenever the gate is bent askew, the spring action becomes soft or stiff, or the body of the krab becomes noticeably gouged, pitch it. And if you ever drop a carabiner even a moderately long ways, invisible fatigue cracks can result which greatly diminish the strength. Most biners are made of aircraft quality, 7000 series aluminum alloy, with a useful life span exceeding 10 years. But effects from normal work hardening can shorten the life span. Metal fatigue is a much-bandied word that is usually misinterpreted. Metal does not get tired. The term metal fatigue actually refers to a crack in the material without any microscopic deformation. And if the carabiner is cracked, you obviously pitch it. Corrosion is the arch foe of aluminum, and manifests in a white powdery dust. Climbers active on sea cliffs should take special note of this. If there's ever any doubt that the carabiner is defective—just pitch it. If you don't, you'll inevitably find yourself at a crux with only one biner left—the dubious one. You'll clip that old, corroded, creaking krab into the anchor and cry a river because you were too cheap or stupid not to have retired a piece of gear whose time was up.

Secure carabiners against unwanted opening:
1. the wrong way
2. gates in opposition

It's not unheard of for a carabiner to mysteriously come open at the worst possibly time. Whenever this is even a remote possibility, use two carabiners and turn them so the gates are opposing—so they can only open in opposite directions. A special "locking" carabiner was designed to safeguard against unwanted opening. It features a threaded or spring loaded sleeve which fits over the mouth of the krab and prohibits opening. Many experienced climbers don't bother with these, for they are not essential gear, and tend to promote false security. If you feel better using one, by all means do so; just remmber, they are no stronger than an ordinary carabiner, they simply prevent unwanted opening, and using two, opposing-gated biners is safer still.

Gaining popularity is the "dogleg", or "bent-gate" biner. The gate is bowed in, and when depressed, gives a wider gate opening than other biners. The real advantage is when you're desperate and eye-to-eye with fixed protection. With the bent-gate krab you can slap the rope into the bowed gate; a little pressure and a jerk and the biner is clipped. Unfortunately, slings can easily bind back on the bowed gate which will open them all too easily. More on these in the next chapter.

Chouinard Equipment has offered this advice per carabiner maintenance: "If gates are a bit sticky, cross pressure on the gate while open can straighten slightly. A dry silicone at the hinge, then blowing clean with gas station hose, works wonders (for gate action). This also works well with the lock ring or sleeve on locking biners. Don't use oil."

There are those occasional times when it is necessary to tie in to the middle of a rope. A third person may want to join a party of two who has only one rope, perhaps. The only

The Butterfly knot

viable knot for this purpose, one that maintains the maximum amount of strength along the length of the line, is the butterfly knot. Naturally, use only doubled carabiners to clip in with, and reverse those gates!

ANCHORS

The ANCHOR is the fail-safe spot to which we attach ourselves; it is the single most important part of the climbing protection system. Normally this is to secure ourselves to the cliff, but not always. Commencing a climb, we may choose to "tie off" (anchor to) a tree or block. Anchors furnished by the terrain are called NATURAL ANCHORS, be they trees, chockstones, horns, or whatever. ARTIFICIAL ANCHORS are provided by specially designed climbing hardware which exploit cracks and hollows in the rock. When the rock is bereft of both natural anchors and cracks, a climber may drill a hole in the rock and place a bolt—a PERMANENT ANCHOR.

Anchors (say a sling wrapped around a tree) which can withstand force from any angle are called MULTIDIREC-TIONAL ANCHORS. Anchors, such as runners over horns or flakes, are only good for downward pull and these are called DIRECTIONAL ANCHORS.

Anchoring to a tree:
1. Incorrect. This stresses the relatively weak gate of the carabiner.
2., 3. Two good ways.

NATURAL ANCHORS

Runners are vital in exploiting natural protection and can be looped around or over anything that can provide a solid anchor: Knobs, spikes, flakes, through blocks, over chockstones, around trees, or other fixed objects. Sometimes it is handy to have a double runner (12 feet, carried in a double loop over your shoulder), though many climbers choose to simply tie or loop two normal length runners together. Runners simply looped over protuberances can be marginal—fine for downward pull, but susceptible to slipping, or being lifted off from lateral pull or rope drag. Whenever possible, tie the knob (or horn, spike, etc.) off by forming a slip knot in the runner, and cinching it snug. With flakes, pull the runner down behind the flake to where it is lodged between the flake and the wall. If all else fails, clip a piece of gear onto the bottom of the runner. A little extra weight does much to keep a runner from simply sliding off.

Slinging a horn with a slip knot on a runner.

Common sense and sober judgement are necessary in determining if a natural anchor is good, or something less. With most climbers, a little experience makes this question pretty cut and dried. You usually know if a chockstone is loose, or whether a sling will slip off a knob, but not always. You wouldn't bother to place an anchor if you didn't need one, so always test the rock or tree or whatever if there are any doubts as to its strength. With potentially loose chockstones or flakes, test them gingerly, lest you pull them off on yourself or someone below.

Also known as chockstones, or simply chocks, nuts are metal wedges of various sizes and designs, strung with cable or rope, which fit into constrictions or cavities in the rock. Except for the more difficult artificial climbs, nuts have all but replaced pitons as the means of securing anchors in the rock. Prior to 1970, pitons were the standard way to obtain anchors. Pitons were originally made of soft iron, and because removal could ruin them, they were usually left "fixed" in the crack. American ingenuity came up with almost indestructable chrome-moly steel pitons around 1958. With these there evolved the American ethic of always removing your pitons, leaving the crack "clean" for the next party, not leaving a string of fixed pitons to aid and mark the way for later ascents. This provided for high adventure and, for those later ascents, a feeling similar to the pioneers who first climbed a route. But the new pitons really brutalized the rock. Repeated placement and removal had ruined more than one climb, leaving huge and unsightly "piton scars"—literally holes blasted into the rock—and nuts came to replace pitons none too soon. To the climber, there is aesthetic allure to a perfect crack rifling into the sky. That we can now climb these without ravishing their form is a testament to how far climbing has come. Nuts cause no damage to the stone; and most climbers find that the modern way of "clean climbing" is a much more artistic and satisfying way to climb than hammering their way to the summit.

Tradition says that the modern chock evolved from the British technique of tying off natural chockstones in the cracks. This led to placing chockstones in the cracks and stringing runners over them. Next came machine nuts (found along the railroad tracks below the British crags) through which rope was slung. Sometime in the sixties someone began making nuts particularly for rock climbing. The first nuts were crude and had limited applications but once the wide use of nuts caught on in the early 1970s, the designs steadily improved to where, now, in most cases, nuts can provide better anchors than driven pitons ever could.

When weighted, a nut will lodge in the narrowing slot in which it is placed. Obviously, a nut is placed with a certain *direction of pull* in mind, usually straight down. In some instances, a nut is placed so the direction of pull is straight out, even straight up (explained later). Whatever the placement, the loop of sling or cable issuing from the nut can be considered an arrow which, when extended from the nut, clearly shows where the direction of pull should be.

Nuts are placed in a wide variety of cracks and hollows, so they come in many shapes and sizes. Still, nuts are basically variations of two themes: TAPERS, or stoppers; and HEXENTRICS, or hexes. Both are designed to slot into constrictions, or bottlenecks in the crack. Placing a sound nut is relatively easy with a little practice, but keep these points in

The direction of pull.

mind: 1) Try and select the nut which best matches the taper of the crack. 2) Set the nut so maximum surface area is on the rock (you don't want the nut lodged on just a few crystals). 3) Remember that usually—but not always—a bigger nut is more secure than a smaller one, if you have a choice. 4) Place the nut no deeper than is necessary to meet the above criteria. To do otherwise only makes removal difficult; it does not make the nut more secure. More tricks used in placing nuts will be further reviewed in the chapter: The Art of Leading. For now, we will examine the different types of nuts.

Tapers

These are made by dozens of different manufacturers, each giving a little different look to the one timeless design. The first tapers were much wider than they were thick. Now, virtually all tapers have adopted a boxier shape, better for several reasons, especially endwise placements. They vary from thumbnail-sized micros strung with what appears to be piano wire, to weighty, inch-and-a-half bombers strung with special "Spectra" cord which, for it's diameter, is "stronger than steel". Originally, all but the smallest tapers were strung with rope. Now, swaged cable has replaced rope for all but the largest-sized tapers. The cable gives us

Tapers

several advantages. It is generally stronger than rope of corresponding size. The stiff cable allows easier placement. Where a taper strung with rope will droop when held, the wired nut is like a knife which can be slotted with one hand; and the stiff cable allows a few inches of extra reach which can sometimes make a serious difference.

Variations on the taper follow four basic patterns: The straight taper; the curved taper; the offset taper; and the micro brass and steel taper.

The straight taper is the original design. Even the smallest ones are stronger than one would think. The wider, or "face sides" are flat, and tapered down at the same angle. These are most useful in a crack whose sides taper uniformly, and where the slot best matches the taper of the nut. A good match means a good fit, and again, a good fit means most of the surface area of the nut is on the rock. A common error is to try and place the biggest taper the crack will accept. Much more important is finding the placement that seats solidly in the crack. The obvious bottleneck leaves little to chance; the nut locks in as if the crack was made for it. But when the crack is flared, or convoluted, or shallow, it often takes some fiddling to find the best placement—or any placement. All but the smallest tapers can be placed endwise as well, so try whatever works best. The better tapers feature slightly beveled edges which makes them easier to both place and remove. The rounded edges also increase purchase in marginal edge contact placements. The wire cable is secured with a swage over which a rubber shrink tube swage cover is secured, holding the loop together. Most manufacturers will in some manner color-code the sizes in its line. With practice, you will learn what color corresponds to what sized nut, and can then grab the right one quickly—a boon when the going's grim.

The curved taper has virtually replaced the straight taper in the medium to large range. One side is concave, the other convex. The theory is that most tapers are placed where the sides of the crack vary slightly. When placed and yanked on, the curved taper does a quasi-camming action on the convex side until it rotates into the best spot. The top of the concave side is milled flat, which with the camming action on the other side results in a three-point foundation once seated. They work especially well when the constriction is gently curved. This sounds like babble, even to me, but simply place a curved taper and all will be clear.

The classic taper

The curved taper can also be placed endwise, both ends forming a straight taper as thick as the next widest nut; so you have the best of both worlds. The curve of the taper varies with each manufacturer. When the curving is less pronounced, they are generally easier to remove.

A useful variation to the taper is the off-set, available only in small sizes, and tapered on all sides, forming an asymmetrical trapezoid. I didn't understand that either. Basically, one edge is thicker than the other—or "offset". (Better get one and look at it) These offsets are perfect for flaring cracks which narrow in the back, in which a straight or curved taper will find scant purchase. Be warned, however, that offsets are less forgiving in marginal placements, and unless you've got most of the surface area firmly locked, offsets can "pop" quicker than you can say "watch me". Originally

Off-set taper

viewed as a specialty item for use on big artificial routes, many free climbers carry a few for those "oddball" placements, where nothing else works quite as well.

Tapers are made in remarkably small sizes, most often "straight taper" in profile. The super thin but strong cable on these tiny nuts is either silver soldered or cast with the nut, resulting in cable strengths that exceed those of the body of the nut. Some are made of hard brass, even stainless steel; others are cast from "investment cast" brass. In a fall, the harder brass and stainless tends to break the surrounding rock away if the rock is poor. The investment brass is somewhat malleable, so it is less likely to break the rock and seats well owing to increased friction and bite. When the rock is diamond hard, the malleable brass taper may deform and shear through the placement, so there's a trade-off involved. Most practiced climbers carry both kinds and vary use according to the need.

A manufacturer of these tiny tapers, Wild Country, offers the following advice: "The limiting factor with small nuts is not their lower strength, but rather their small surface area which concentrates the impact of a fall so intensely that when they fail, it is likely because they rip out, not through broken wires." Be aware, though, that with long use, the cable usually frays beneath the head of the nut.

There are other modifications on the taper that you'll see as well. The faces of some of the smaller tapers have been gouged out to form a teardrop cutaway, or a scoop. This supposedly adds purchase when the nut is placed between a cluster of crystals. Other tapers have been filed this way and that, are banana shaped, squat, tall, titanium, plastic, even wooden. But they all work by being slotted into a constriction and weighted in the direction of the cable.

Hexentrics

Hexentrics

Six-sided and barrel shaped, hexentrics—or simply "hexes"—are good for wide cracks, bottlenecks, and when the crack is more suited for a round, as opposed to a tapered nut. The sides are shaped so they can be wedged in three different attitudes, camming fairly well even in parallel-sided cracks. Placed endwise, both ends are tapered, and the hex is slotted like a big taper. Since Chouinard Equipment introduced them in 1971 they have steadily evolved. The newest batch feature angled sidewalls for better endwise placements.

Since the introduction of Spring Loaded Camming Devices (SLCDs), hexes, long the only viable nut for wide cracks, have almost disappeared, but not altogether. For the true bottleneck placement, a bomber hex is still the strongest nut in town. Not one has ever broken in use. They are relatively inexpensive, and many times can find better purchase than any high tech SLCDs. Consequently, most climbers carry a selection on their rack. Ten sizes.

Hexentrics, placed as a chock (left), and as a cam (right).

Lowe Tri-cams

Many climbers have considered this odd-looking nut just a piece of esoterica, but some climbers swear by them. The design creates a tripod with two parallel camming rails flat against one side of the crack or pocket, and the fulcrum point on the other. They're uniquely good in horizontal placements, providing both cam and wedging action. Tri-cams also work well in desert sandstone, the point digging into the soft rock. In certain shallow pocket placements, they have no peer. Eleven sizes.

Tri-cams, placed as a chock (left), and as a cam (right).

Stringing your nuts

All but the smallest hexes and tapers are made to accept a length of rope rather than a swaged cable. This is particularly useful in hexentrics because it allows an unrestricted camming action of the nut. Originally, both tapers and hexentrics were strung with various dimensions of nylon rope. Once Kevlar cord hit the market, everyone shifted to it because it proved to be much stronger than nylon of the same size and it wore well. Presently, most nuts machined to accept cordage have holes drilled for the standard 5.5mm Kevlar line. Now, however, new accessory cords are being produced that are sure to replace Kevlar, being both stronger and more wear resistant. Spectra, a special form of polyethylene, is incredibly strong for its size. Gemini, a blend of Spectra and Kevlar, allows light and durable use of the otherwise slippery Spectra. Both fiber blends are available in 5.5mm for chock cord and in flat stock for runners and quick draws.

Use the double fisherman's to secure the cord because it is a knot that is relatively permanent. Keep the knot near the carabiner end of the loop so that it does not interfere with the nut placement and, by its stiffness, tends to keep the loop open to accept a biner readily.

Removing Nuts

Removing, or "cleaning" nuts is sometimes no mean feat, especially if they've been fallen on. The best strategy in cleaning any nut is to first examine the placement with an eye toward simply reversing the path by which the nut was placed. Sometimes, just a tap with a carabiner can jar a set nut free. If the nut cannot be wiggled loose and lifted out, a moderate upward jerk will often free it.

If the nut is buried deep in a crack, you may have to really yard on it. Be warned that this can bend any cable which, done repeatedly, can not only ruin the nut's symmetry but weaken the cable; and you can actually break the cable on the smaller tapers. Always keep an eye peeled for frays in the cable, especially around the swage, and above the holes in the top of the nut. The broken strand not only diminishes strength, but can prick the fingers something ferocious. When this occurs, just pitch them. On cabled nuts, the taper will sometimes float around on the cable, making cleaning difficult. A practical solution is to fill the drill holes in the nut with epoxy, which permanently fixes the taper where it should be. You can push in on the placement with the epoxied cable to help pluck the nut. In addition, the last thing you'll enjoy when hanging off a one-finger rugosity is trying to shove an unepoxied nut to the correct end of the wire loop. However, on rare occasions you may want to slide the nut to the middle so the cable can be used as an extension loop. Can't have it both ways. Best is to epoxy some of your nuts, and leave some alone.

As an aid to tapping out well-lodged nuts, cleaning tools are made in a dozen different forms, all thin and blade-shaped and all invaluable in cleaning a lodged taper. A little experimentation will show just how to pry and tap out stubborn nuts. With visions of a shiv buried in their belly, some climbers are loath to carry what is essentially a blunt knife, fearing a fall might somehow result in a puncture from the cleaning tool. Though I've never once heard of this happening, more than a few climbers are not looking to be first. Whatever, tapers are often left on climbs when a cleaning tool would more often than not have gotten the nut free.

SPRING LOADED CAMMING DEVICES

In 1967, Greg Lowe invented the first camming device for protecting rock climbs. Greg's version was a bust, but it got the concept out there. Finally, in 1978, Ray Jardine started marketing "Friends", and climbing has never been the same.

Friends work so well that when they first came out many past rock masters thought they were a means of cheating. Climbs which for twenty years were feared owing to poor protection were now reduced to mere physical endeavors. Friends had taken the horror right out of them, for you could place a Friend whenever you wanted, and the placement was generally bomber. No longer did a climber cast off on a rugged lead hoping he could get in good nuts, and hoping the nuts were somewhere near the crux. Now you could throw in a Friend whenever you chose, whenever the going got tough. And they were dead easy to place. Gone forever were the days when a climber was greasing out of an overhanging crack, trying to wiggle a hex in where the crack just wouldn't have it and there was no going on without it.

The great benefit of SLCDs is that the crack need not constrict to afford a placement. In fact, a parallel-sided crack is where a SLCD is best placed and where all other nuts fail to work even remotely as well. Since Friends first hit the market, they have been copied by everyone with a machine shop: Now there are Amigos, Camalots, Micromates, Buddies, and others. Some, like Micromates, are designed specifically for thin cracks. They have three, rather than four cams (Three-Cam Units, or TCUs), and their lower profile allows a better range of protection in narrow cracks and pockets. Camalots feature a double axis for the cams, resulting in a wider range of application for SLCDs of the same size. Flexible Friends supplant the rigid stem with a cable stem, giving it a lower profile for thin cracks, and making it far better for horizontal placements. Still, SLCDs all work on the same principal.

Chouinard Camalot in a typical parallel-sided placement.

The manufacturer of the Friends, Wild Country, has offered the following advice regarding SLCDs, but the advice is so sound that it applies to all protection. Parentheses are mine. "The security of climbing protection has always depended on the experience and knowledge of the climber placing it. Climbing hardware is only a tool, and knowledge about how the tool works properly is important to achieving it's greatest performance. With this knowledge, if you have to make a risky gear placement, you'll do so out of intelligence and not out of ignorance. Per SLCDs: Always align stem and cams in the direction of loading (i.e., direction of pull). Don't offset the cams—they have little holding power that way. Realign the cams evenly. Avoid a "tipped" placement, where the cams are placed wide open, and rocking on the cam tips. Always use a sling long enough to ensure you won't move the SLCD by climbing past it. (All SLCDs have the tendency to either "walk" in, or walk out of the crack when even nominal rope drag is pulling on them. A sling connected to the end of the SLCD alleviates the problem.) Don't allow the cams to invert—inverted cams won't hold. Don't stuff a "too large" SLCD into an undersized placement, it may make removal difficult. (It may make removal impossible. Ideally, the cams should be placed at mid range. You must reduce the cam ratio to pull out the SLCD. If you force the SLCD into an undersized placement, you've torqued the cams to their minimum displacement. Since they are spring loaded, the cams are never passive so you can't simply slide the SLCD out and you have no way of reducing the profile any further because it's already at it's minimum so you've just lost an expensive piece of gear.) Never place a rigid stem SLCD so that the stem is not aligned with the direction of pull. Referring to placements when the stem is not in the direction of pull: Bottoming cracks should be avoided as they make cleaning (removal) difficult and may hinder stem alignment during a fall. Flexible Friends will work in such positions, but stems aligned in the direction of pull are always more secure. (And what happens when you encounter a flared or bottoming crack and you can't avoid it? You try and place a taper or a hex. If impossible, you place a SLCD with a flexible shaft and hope it doesn't rip out.) Always regard flexible stems as less predictable than rigid stems. ("Predictable" here means the rigid stem SLCDs rip out less frequently when fallen on.) Four camming surfaces are generally more secure than three. (Sometimes the crack is too shallow to "sink" the SLCD, so one or more cams are hanging out of the crack. Such placements are very suspect.)

1. Incorrect use of a rigid-stem Friend in a horizontal placement risks shearing the stem.
2. Much safer is to use a flexible-stem unit.

The twin-axle Camalots are the only SLCDs that can be used as a passive chock.

These remarks apply to all SLCDs, save for one. Chouinard's Camalots can be placed in their fully open, or "umbrella" configuration—essentially placed like a hex. A hex will generally be better here, but the Camalot has this capacity. Other SLCDs do not.

Sliders, Rock 'n Rollers, etc.

There is a last, specialized genre of protection that combines aspects of the taper and the SLCD. They all share some form of inverted taper that is fixed to a cable. A second taper, inverted the other way, slides up and down the face of the first taper, controlled by a spring loaded cable. Owing to the sliding taper, the device has a variable range and can conform to the exact dimensions of the placement. In rather fast-paced evolution, the first of these units, Sliders, have led to Quickies, Rock 'n Rollers, and Loweballs, among others. Though this is esoteric and specialized equipment, they all work like magic in narrow, shallow, parallel-sided fissures.

A million words and as many photos are both poor substitutes for grabbing a handful of nuts and going to a crag to practice placing them. Find several cracks at ground level and experiment to find how the aforementioned principals work, how to spot the best placements and learn what nut best fits where. Clip a runner into them, step on them, pull on them, discover just how good, or bad, they are. And don't expect expertise in an afternoon. Better than twenty years have gone into refining the modern nut, and statistically, an experienced climber not given to rashness has little chance of hurting himself. But there is no sport on the face of the earth less forgiving to him who makes a major mistake or

From top to bottom:

Lowe Tri-cam, LoweBall, a couple of cleaning tools.

LoweBall in use

oversight in regard to safety. You can get killed in a real hurry by ignoring any aspect of proper climbing. So when it comes time to test your own judgement on whether or not a nut is good, whether you should trust your life to it, do so only after you feel confident you can make the right decision. And the only way for a novice to gain this confidence is to practice nutcraft where it doesn't count—near the ground.

Wide Crack Anchors

The BigBro is available in sizes to fit up to a 12-inch crack

Wide cracks—those over four or five inches—have traditionally proved difficult to provide anchorage. Large "tube" chocks that appeared in the early seventies replaced the huge pitons that hithero had provided a semblance of security. The tubes required a slight constriction to work well, however, and with the introduction of Friends, backyard machine shops produced monster Friends. Now commercially available as Big Dudes, these SLCDs, while heavy, bulky, and certainly expensive, still provide the the best security in the wider cracks. Relatively new on the scene is the BigBro, an extendable tube that works best in parallel-sided cracks, is incredibly strong, compact, and less costly. A push button releases the spring-loaded inner sleeve, the tube is bridged across to both sides of the crack, a threaded ring is spun to lock it all to size, and a sling on one end provides the means to clip in.

PITONS

Pitons (or "pins", or "pegs") are steel devices, usually spike shaped, which are hammered into cracks to secure anchors. The shapes are many, but every modern piton has an eye through which a carabiner is clipped. A recreational climber today might frequent a popular sport climbing area for five years and never hear the ring of a piton being driven. Chocks and SLCDs have made pitons unnecessary in almost all cases. But for big artificial climbs, and now and again in free climbing, pitons still have their place. Regardless, the ranks of climbers experienced in placing pitons is shrinking, and the number of accidents as a result of misplaced trust in fixed piton anchors shows the need for developing pitoning skills.

Prior to World War II, pitons were made of malleable soft iron so they could conform to the crack. Even one placement would maul their shape, and they were usually left in situ, or "fixed", since removal would destroy them. The most common soft steel piton today's climber will run across is the ring-angle, a pin of channel design with welded ring. Obviously these are very old, and in addition to being of suspect security, the welded ring is of such design to fail at relatively low loads. There really is no practical way to test such pitons you may come across on the cliffs; better to assume them to be worthless.

In 1946, a Swiss expatriate named John Salathe hand tooled pegs from Model-T axle stock for the first ascent of Lost Arrow Spire in Yosemite Valley. Tradition says these Salathe pins were the first ever made from hard steel. In the fifties, Chuck Wilts invented the "knife-blade", a wafer-thin peg he fashioned from chrome molybdenum ("chrome-moly") steel. Like Salathe's, these hard steel pins could withstand repeated placement and removal, enabling climbers to scale multi-day climbs with a limited selection, rather than lugging a duffel bag full of soft iron. In the late fifties, Yvon Chouinard began manufacturing chrome moly pitons in his back yard. He quickly expanded and by the early sixties any climber could purchase state-of-the-art chrome-moly pitons. That the first ascent of Yosemite's mightiest walls corresponded with the availability of good pitons was no fluke. While every other facet of climbing technology has steadily evolved, pitons have changed little in the last twenty five years—neither in design or construction. Chouinard had it down by 1962.

Various European manufacturers still market pitons, but in the United States, Chouinard has totally locked this limited market, and is the only company making them on any kind of scale. Chouinard makes pitons in four different shapes. Each model is either stamped or forged of alloy steel, and, for better or worse, all are far more enduring than the hardest granite.

As mentioned, pitons are virtually never used in sport climbing. The one exception is climbers making first ascents. It is rare even for them to use them, but in the case of a hole or a thin, parallel-sided crack, sometimes only a piton can secure the desired protection. To preserve the rock and avoid future climbers having to place the piton, it is always left fixed. Never remove a piton from an established free climb. It's there for a reason. To adequately judge the security of a fixed piton, however, one must have experience in placing them, and a hammer. Most piton hammers have a forged steel head attached to a wooden handle which absorbs the vibrations better than a metal handle. Hammers weigh in around 24 ounces and last for many years.

Pick the piton whose shape best corresponds to the crack. Insert the piton by hand. Ideally it should enter about 75 percent of it's length before you start hammering. Drive it to the hilt. As you hammer it home, a rising ring—like a scale on a xylophone—usually means a sound piton. When you've the choice between placements in a horizontal and vertical crack, the horizontal peg is often better. In such horizontal placements the eye of the piton should always be positioned down. When placing pitons straight up, use the longest pin that will fit. These placements are often better than you would think.

To remove the pin, knock the piton back and forth along the axis of the crack as far as it will go until it's loose, then snatch it as it loosens. If the pin is stubborn and requires extensive hammering to remove, clip a sling into the eye so if it comes out while hammering, you won't drop it. If it's loose, yet still won't come out, try prying with the hammer pick through the eye.

Since the unnecessary use of pitons is frowned upon in virtually every climbing area, how does one practice their use? Basic pitoning is a pretty straightforward technique, but you should try your hand before heading onto a climb where you expect to place them. Most climbing areas have rock outcrops which, owing to poor rock or whatever, no one climbs on. Often times such cliffs are some distance from the central climbing area, which is all the better. Any scrappy crag will do, so long as it has some cracks in it. Find some privacy and experiment.

BOLTS

When there are no cracks for traditional nuts or pitons, a climber can retreat, ignore the need for an anchor and simply "go for it", or he can drill a hole into the blank stone and hammer in a bolt—a permanent anchor.

The use of bolts is the most controversial issue in the climbing game. Most climbers have the intuitive understanding that artistic climbing is to follow a weakness up a given cliff. You work with what nature has given you. There is something inherently distasteful about changing the medium to fit our need, and bolting does just that. Bolting has been called "the murder of the impossible" because with the bolt, you can climb anything, anywhere. We can hammer one in the underside of a glass-smooth ceiling if we want to. But should we? We clear the land because we need a place to hang our hat. But we don't need to climb. We choose to. So what do we do when we come across an otherwise unclimbable section of rock? It has always been a question when the rock, in it's natural state, is either unclimbable or too dangerous to try, whether it's okay to permanently alter it—by placing a bolt—so that we can climb it Well, that depends....

Say there is a 2,000-foot crack that blanks out for thirty feet. Surely it is okay to drill a few bolts for the blank stretch if it means putting together a 2,000-foot classic. But what if the blank section is 100 feet long and requires 8 bolts? What if the blank section is 1,000 feet long and requires 80 bolts? And what if all 2,000 feet are blank? And what if the 2,000-foot wall is 65 degrees and would tender a face climb of the first order if we only took the time to install the requisite

Bolts of various types: The two contraction-type bolts at the bottom of the picture at left are typical of the $1/4$-inch anchors found on many routes. They clearly are not as strong or durable as the modern $3/8$-inch bolts pictured. Carabiner for scale.

bolts—say 230. Bolting is compromising the rock—there's no way around that. So where do we draw the line? Should we draw the line?

This is a philosophical question that the beginner need not face but should be aware of from the start. The question is reserved for those who make first ascents—the first people to establish a climbing route. For these pioneers, the excitement of discovery has motivated climbers since the first man stood on top of the first mountain. As today's pacesetters look ever harder for new lines, they increasingly face the bolting question. This is not the venue to pass judgement on the pros and cons of bolting. Climbing's allure is that everyone is left to decide for himself. There are no governing bodies, thank God. The flip side is that when a climber places a bolt he impacts the world of all climbers for all time.

The bolt has been an integral part of American climbing for over fifty years. Many of America's best climbs have dozens of bolts. Most face climbs wouldn't exist, or would be suicidal, without bolt anchors. As you get immersed in climbing you will quickly learn how bolts are "at once a blessing and a curse", as Yosemite legend Royal Robbins said. For now, let's see just what they are and how they work.

First is the hole. This is drilled by hammering on a drill bit held by a rolled steel sleeve/holder. By hammering the holder and twisting it at the same time, the hole is accomplished, taking up to a half hour for a $1^1/_2$-inch deep hole drilled in hard granite—even longer in dense limestone. For years this tedious drilling deterred excessive bolting, but the introduction of lightweight battery-fed electric drills has changed all that, with thirty seconds for a hole.

For decades, the $^1/_4$-inch diameter bolt was standard. As more and more of these sheared off unexpectedly, the $^3/_8$-inch bolt has come to replace the old $^1/_4$ inchers. The bolt is nail-like, and may be of several types: The contraction bolt has a split flange which is squeezed together as it's driven in the narrow hole. The expansion bolt expands a surrounding sleeve as it is either driven in, or after it is set, by wrenching down the head. Some of the best bolt anchors simply combine a threaded bolt with epoxy that is stronger than the rock.

Carabiners can then be clipped to the bolt hanger, a strip of bent metal that is usually secured by a nut screwed onto the bolt. Other bolts are like normal machine bolts, and the hanger is already affixed when the bolt is driven home. Most of the new $^3/_8$-inch bolts have a minimum strength of 4,000 pounds, but the older, $^1/_4$-inch bolts hold significantly less.

A beginner should not worry about the mechanics of placing a bolt. You never place bolts on existing routes, so you'll never need that "skill" until you're an expert doing first ascents; and many experts never do first ascents. For general sport climbing you need only know how to judge the condition of a bolt on an existing route. There is no absolutely reliable way to test in situ bolts, but plenty of reasons to want to. Here are some suggestions:

Always consider a $^1/_4$-inch bolt suspect. They are no longer placed as anchors, though they are commonly found on existing routes, and any you come across are bound to be old.

Make sure the hanger is flush to the wall, not a "spinner", where the hanger spins around. This means the hole was drilled too shallow for the bolt stud. And don't try to "fix" the spinner by hammering on it. Had that been possible the first party would have sunk it. Further hammering will only damage the shank and the head. So never hit an existing bolt with a hammer.

Commercially-made hangers are made of stainless steel, good for over 4,000 pounds. Beware of home-made hangers. Most are fashioned from inferior aluminum angle stock, prone to work-hardening, eventual brittleness, and failure.

If the bolt is a "screw-head", make sure the nut is snug and the threads are in good shape. If the threads are severely denuded or stripped, the nut has little resistance and can pop off under surprisingly low impact force. If the bolt is a "buttonhead" or looks like a machine bolt, again see if it's snugly set, and free of fatigue cracks.

If the bolt is bent, or looks to be set in an oblique hole, be very suspicious of it's strength. Rust is another thing to look for. Discoloration is natural enough, but a lot of rust denotes a "coffin nail", and you know what those are used for.

Use common sense. If the bolt looks funky, don't trust it. And always back up a bolt with a nut if possible. A perfect bolt is nearly impossible to pull out, even from an astronomical fall. But be careful: there's a lot of bad bolts out there.

HOW SAFE ARE THOSE FIXED ANCHORS?

Besides bolts, many popular climbs have fixed nuts and/or pitons. Gear is expensive, so the gear usually was not left on purpose, but because someone couldn't remove it. But not always. Fatigue, terror, and inexperience often keep a person from really trying to clean a stubborn nut. So never trust them outright. With nuts, first check the placement. Is it good? If so, has the nut been mauled by greedy hammers? Has the cable been torn by people trying to force it out? If it checks out, it's probably okay, but back it up anyway.

Inspect all fixed pitons closely. A piton which Herman Munster couldn't clean with a nine-pound sledge becomes, after the winter freeze and thaw, loose as a tent stake in peat. Check that it's firmly placed. To test a fixed piton well, a piton hammer is a necessity; a couple good blows along the axis of the crack will give good indication of how tightly it has been placed. Follow up with blows to set the pin. Keeping in mind that few climbers test fixed pitons, either carry a hammer, test the pin inadequately with blows from the heaviest nut you have, or treat the fixed pin as worthess; it probably is! Often the eye is cracked, and if you can't back it up, it's a judgement call. Sometimes larger fixed angles will be more secure if treated like a chockstone and wrapped with sling. If you know a route features a lot of fixed pitons, carrying a hammer and testing the pitons is the only way to intelligently gauge your security.

An aged bolt anchor placed in rock soft enough for the wind to quickly erode. Obviously someone was foolish enough to use this for an anchor.

Dan Langmade photo

Fixed SLCDs are rare but not unheard of. The cheapest ones are 30 dollars so everyone and his brother has probably tried to clean it. Make sure the sling or cable is in good shape before trusting it.

Fixed slings should never be trusted blindly; hidden damage may spell disaster for anyone who does not instead examine what the sling is attached to and re-rig the anchor accordingly. Most climbers try to clean fixed slings just to get that trash off the cliff.

The double overhand

You must first uncoil, or "flake out", the rope. Find the end, then feed out the line in a neat stack, making sure not to bury the end. You now have a bottom and top of the pile, and, to avoid tangles, you always draw the rope from the top. Now you're at the bottom of the cliff, harnessed, booted up, tied into the rope and chomping at the bit, but you have to rig a bombproof anchor before the climb starts. You look for a natural anchor—a stout tree or a large block. You could use the rope to tie these off, but you'll go with slings. Better to get tree sap on a two dollar piece of webbing than the rope. And the anchor is often weighted, pulled on, jerked about, so you'll let the sling take any abuse. The rope is plenty strong for this, but why scuff it up if you don't have to.

Once you have arranged a natural anchor, you must tie into it. Since you are already tied into the end of the rope, you must use a knot for the middle of the rope—a "middleman's" knot. The butterfly knot mentioned earlier, while ideal for a climber tying into the middle of a rope, is too cumbersome to tie and untie for use as a tie-in to the anchor. For that purpose, two knots, the double overhand and the double figure-eight, provide the strength and ease of tying to make their use exclusive of any other for the main tie-in to the anchor. The double overhand is the simplest knot imaginable, but once weighted can be a struggle to untie. Better is the double-figure eight—strong and easy to untie.

The double figure-eight

Knot now in hand, be certain *never* to tie off an anchor with only one carabiner. That is simply relying too much on a piece of equipment that can easily hide flaws. Besides which, the gate might get torqued open by a bight of rope. A slim chance, granted, but you won't be taking any chances so you use two carabiners, gates opposed.

If there is no substantial natural anchor—a tree, block, or large bush—you must construct an artificial anchor using nuts. The first rule with anchors is never use only one nut. *Never.* Most experienced climbers don't consider an anchor secure until they have set a minimum of three good nuts.

Multi-nut Anchors

Constructing a multi-nut anchor will at first take some time and trouble, but a trained eye and the knack for finding propitious nut slots—both a result of experience—quickly make this routine. Climbers are called on to do this many times each outing, so the training comes quickly.

A tie-in knot that is quick and easy to tie, easy to adjust for length once it is tied, and unties easily is naturally a knot to be welcomed by climbers. Such a knot is the clove hitch. It is particularly useful in constructing multi-nut anchors. While the trade off to all this utility is less strength than other knots, the wise climber simply uses a double figure-eight somewhere in the anchor system. The clove hitch probably should not be used as the sole tie-in knot.

Vertical Cracks

The clove hitch

First locate a placement which, by itself, looks absolutely bombproof, preferably in a medium to wide crack. Once you have set it, you build the anchor around it. Make sure that this first, bombproof nut is not too isolated, not the only nut slot around. Ideally, the anchor should be rigged in a small area—say three feet of crack. This way it is much easier to tie everything off, is easy to keep an eye on, and is generally less complicated and neater.

Once you have that first nut set, you must set a nut in OPPOSITION to it, so the direction of pull is opposite to your first, bombproof nut. Your first nut will be for downward pull, so you must find a bombproof placement for upward pull. The oppositional nut, when combineded with it's counterpart, provides a multi-directional anchor, one you can weight in any direction. And *all anchors must be mult-directional.* On small stances you will want to rig the anchor so at least some of the nuts are above your waist. By being

Using a clove hitch to tie two nuts in opposition.

clever with your tie-in you can use the upper nuts to lean comfortably off while also maintaining a taut tie-in below.

SLCDs are very useful in rigging anchors because you can jockey the SLCD around to an ideal location, rather than hoping for bottlenecks or constrictions in the right place.

Many climbers favor a "two down, two up" configuration: Two nuts for downward pull, two nuts in opposition for upward pull. Many times any one of these nuts would hold well enough, but it's the no-doubt-about-it anchor that gives us peace of mind, so we always strive to make it so.

Horizontal Cracks

Depending on the cliff, at least some of the time we're left to rig anchors in horizontal cracks. At least part of the system is built on opposing placements, where the direction of pull is toward the middle. But often the best single nut is the one set for a direct, outward pull. With a taper or hex, you find a slot, wiggle the nut in, and move it horizontally to where the lip of the crack is narrower than the depths. When pulled straight out, the rock would have to break away for the nut to fail. Of course SLCDs have simplified this process, for you only need a reasonable crack to arrange the anchor as you see fit.

Opposing nuts rigged with a sling tied into a clove hitch.

Equalizing the Anchor

Once you have set the nuts, the safest method is to equalize the system so any and all force is distributed evenly between the various placements. Very often, however,

Self-equalizing slider knot. Remember to double up the tie-in carabiner!

anchors are rigged whereby one set of opposing nuts provides a backup for another set of opposing nuts but, though both sets are tied securely together, strictly speaking they are not perfectly equalized. The most common modes of tying off the anchor are these:

1) Tying off the nuts with the rope, usually in combination with clove hitches, 2) Tying the nuts off with a sling, using

clove hitches, then tying into the sling; or, 3) equalizing the anchor with a self-equalizing "sliding knot", and clipping into the sling. And once the anchor is all set up, apply some tension in the direction of pull and scrutinize it like an engineer. Often you will want to make some small, finishing adjustments to get the system just as you want it. All components of the anchor should have all the slack removed, usually accomplished by cinching up the clove hitches. More elaborate methods of equalizing an anchor are possible; these listed are the most common modes.

A Few Thoughts

The anchor is the foundation of safe climbing. A poor anchor is like jogging on the freeway—you won't last long. There is no mystery to rigging a sound one. If there is ever any doubt, double up the anchor. While three nuts are often adequate, it's not uncommon to see an anchor with four, even five nuts, all equalized. When the crack is thin, forcing the use of smaller cabled tapers, place more rather than less. Trusting an anchor rigged completely from micro nuts is petrifying duty, and should only happen in extreme emergencies, never out of choice. SLCDs have proven their utility, but many climbers avoid rigging anchors completely from mechanical devices, particularly for top-rope situations, where the weighting and unweighting can cause the SLCD to walk around. There's nothing like a bomber "passive" (non-mechanical) nut buried in a bottleneck. Come hell or high water, that nut's going nowhere. There are situations in climbing where you may take a calculated risk, but never with the anchor.

THE BELAY

As the leader climbs, the second man feeds out the rope, or, "belays". Both his anchor and location are generically called "the belay", or "belay station". You climb in stages called "pitches", which usually refers to the distance between belay stations, something less than a ropelength. A pitch is rarely a whole ropelength, however, for you often stop short at a ledge, a good stance or crack which offers a convenient place to belay. A bombproof anchor is far more important than stretching a lead out simply to make it longer. This only wastes time, for in passing obvious belay stances, you are often left to squander time constructing an anchor in a poor crack or at an awkward locale.

Belaying is the technique of not only paying out the rope, but holding it fast should your partner fall. The entire protection system of rock climbing depends on the certainty of both the belay anchor and the belayer to do their job: to stop the climber should he fall, and to remain fastened to the cliff. It is very rare that both the belay and anchor should fail and it's into the beyond if they do. That is why extreme vigilance is always paid to both the anchor and belay. A cavalier attitude toward their importance will get someone killed in a hurry. The process is fundamental and the technique is simple and reliable. Still, 40 percent of all fatal climbing accidents in Yosemite were due to mistakes and failures in the belay chain. Consequently, the importance of a sound belay system cannot be overstated.

The Body Belay

It is always best to learn climbing techniques using the simplest methods first, advancing to more complex equipment and techniques once we've mastered the basics, and the basic belay is the body, or "hip" belay. There are two ends of the rope: your end, which you are tied into and

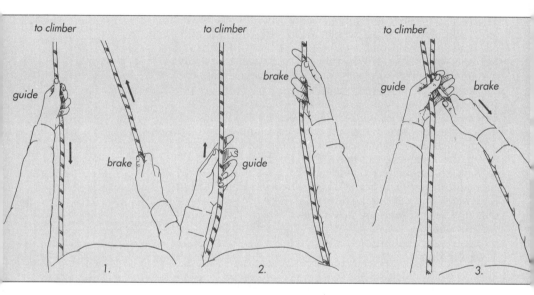

THE BODY BELAY:

Taking rope in:

1. Both hands grasped tightly, the rope is fed around the back.
2. The guide hand slides up,
3. clasps both ends of the rope above the other hand to allow the brake hand to slide down and begin the series again.

which is tied off to the anchor, and the "live" end, which goes to the person climbing, the person you are belaying. The rope is wrapped around your waist and grasped firmly in each hand. The "live" end going to the climber is handled by the "guide" hand. The "brake" hand holds the rope on your other side. When the climber is leading away from you, the guide hand feeds the rope out, pulling it around your waist and through the brake hand on your other side; when the climber is ascending up to you, the guide hand pulls in the slack as the climber ascends. As the rope is reeled in, it passes around your back to the brake hand which, too, is pulling in slack—the brake hand pulling the rope away, the guide hand pulling it toward you, always keeping the rope snug around your back.

Belaying a climber leading away from you is fairly simple: The guide hand shuffles out the rope in little tugs, the payed-out rope moving smoothly around your back and through the brake hand on the other side. Taking the rope up, or belaying a climber "in" is a little tricky at first, and involves a three part sequence. The guide hand is extended away from the waist. It clasps the rope and pulls it in. Simultaneously, the brake hand is pulling out, clasping the rope and pulling it away from your body as it passes around your waist. That's the first stroke: The guide hand pulls in, the brake hand pulls out. At the end of that stroke, the guide hand is at your side, and the brake hand extended out from your waist. Part two requires the brake hand to momentarily hold fast while the guide hand slides back out along the live end. When the arm is fully extended, the guide—still holding the rope on that side—reaches across and grabs the brake hand rope above the brake hand. Part three involves the brake hand sliding back to your side, and the process is repeated: Guide hand pulls in, brake hand pulls out. Guide hand extends,

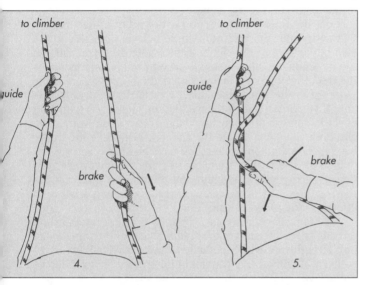

THE BODY BELAY

4. Letting rope out.
5. The braking action: the brake hand wraps the rope around the waist.

grabs both sides, brake hand slides back. This procedure sounds complicated but is very simple to perform. It is the only way to belay and still observe the golden rule: The brake hand *never* leaves the rope. Not only does it never leave the rope, your fingers are always curled around it, ready to clench hard when necessary. A fall is checked by the brake hand moving across your waist to the opposite hip. When you try to belay the rope in, never letting your brake hand leave the clenched position, you'll see there is only one way to do so—the way just described.

The ability to stop a falling climber depends on several things. You must not be caught unaware. Your attention must remain focused on the climber with whose life you are entrusted. When a climber falls, your brake hand must quickly come across your waist to the opposite hip, so the rope makes a complete loop around your hips. The friction is increased dramatically this way, and most falls can be held with little effort. In time, this reaction will become instinctive. You must be properly braced, anticipating both the impact force and the direction of pull caused by the falling climber. But all of this is of little value if you are not properly anchored. To say it again: the anchor is the backbone of the safety system. It, beyond anything, *must* be secure!

When you start a climb, the belayer should be located close to, if not right at, the base of the rock, and tied taut to the belay anchor. If there is any slack between belayer and anchor, a long fall may jerk the belayer off his feet and thrash him around until he comes taut to the anchor, while the rope can be ripped from his hands, resulting in disaster. Every fall generates force in one direction—the DIRECTION OF PULL. Always station yourself in direct line between the direction of pull and the anchor. If you don't, the force of the fall may drag you there anyway, and you might forfeit the belay—and the leader's life—during the flight.

Consider these examples. You're tied off to a huge tree ten feet away from the cliff, and you're belaying ten feet to the side of the start of the climb. If the leader falls, you can plot the direction of pull as a straight line from his first anchor to the tree. If you are not in line with that pull—if you are some ways off to the side—the impact will, perforce, drag you in line. If you are in line, but have tied the anchor off with a lot of slack, you will probably be dragged toward, or even up the cliff until you come taut to the anchor. Meanwhile the leader has fallen that much farther. You have no stance and are left to hold the belay while bouncing over the ground or after getting banged against the cliff—and the sudden force can rip the rope free. If you're set up correctly, catching a fall is an effortless and routine event.

If you must arrange your anchor on the cliff, try and rig it directly below the start of the climb. This puts the direction of pull straight up, which is far less awkward than having to compensate for a belay coming in from the side which forces the belayer into an oblique angle. The stance is of key importance to a ground belay rigged on the cliff—that, and a taut tie-off to the anchor. The short tie-off keeps you from being lifted off the ground. Since a fall will draw you toward the cliff, many climbers like to keep one leg braced against the wall, acting as a shock absorber in the event of a fall.

There is a remote chance that the rope can be lifted over your back—if the guide hand is somehow jerked loose from the rope. A "guiding biner" solves this. Clip a biner into your swami belt or harness near the guide hand. The live end is then taken up or paid out through the biner, and even if the guide hand comes loose, the line still goes around the back to the brake hand. You will quickly learn that the guide hand is no more than a guide and does little to stop the fall. It's the friction around the waist and the brake hand coming across the opposite hip that accomplish the brake.

When the pull is straight up, many climbers pass the rope under their butt instead of around their waist. Even with the guide biner, the straight up pull will often draw the rope up one's back, which is quite sensitive and fairly lean. So your bottom—with the rope running under it—is a better and more secure cushion when belaying for the upward pull. In any event, always wear a shirt, and keep it tucked in unless you want some "galley slave"-like scars.

On paper, the body belay sounds both strenuous and painful, and it's easy to envision a long fall sawing you in half or striping you with bone-deep rope burns. Neither will happen. Much of the impact force is absorbed by the rope, which stretches quite a bit, by the equipment the rope is running through, by the belay anchor, and finally, by the belayer. And the friction afforded by your back or bottom, plus the natural dampening of your body is such that—if the system is rigged and executed correctly—a small housewife can hold a baker's apprentice on the biggest fall he could take.

ANALYZING A
BELAY STATION:

1, 2. Two sets of opposing nut anchors, secured with clove hitches, except

3. Figure-eight knot, for maximum security.

4. Belayer's brake hand.

5. Guiding biner attached to the harness holds the leader's end of the rope in place.

6. The direction of pull should the leader fall.

7. The tie-in from the waist goes down to a non-directional anchor. (Ideally, the belayer should be in a direct line between this anchor tie-in and the direction of pull so that she does not get pulled out of place should the leader fall. Here, as oftentimes happens, the anchors lie to the side of the belayer's stance.

Beginners frequently develop a penchant for belaying one way, always using the same brake hand. Situations arise which will require you to belay with one hand or the other, so practice belaying both ways from the start.

The body belay has been described as a "dynamic" belay in several recent articles and manuals, and this is a misnomer. Years ago, when the old hemp ropes would snap under high impacts, several authorities suggested letting a little rope intentionally slip through the hands to ease the shock on the hemp—a true "dynamic" belay. I'd wager this was never accomplished, though, because once the rope gets to speed the hands haven't been made that can simply crimp it to a stop. The recent re-invention of the term "dynamic belay" simply refers to inherent give in the system, and in no way harks back to the diabolical suggestion of letting some line smoke through your hands in a misguided attempt to ease the fall.

Belay Devices

A belay using a belay device is now commonly called a "static" belay, as the rope is locked tight in the device in the event of a fall (several of the devices actually let a few inches of the rope slip through them before they lock). The same rules apply when using a belay device as they do with a body belay: you still have a guide and brake hand, and the latter never leaves the rope. The rest—taut to the anchor, in line with the direction of pull, staying alert and braced—is all the same, save that the device, rather than your back and brake hand, provides the friction, or stopping power. Since most belay devices are normally clipped to the front of a harness or swami belt, the term "static belay" is really hogwash. The rope is indeed locked fast in the device when stopping a fall, but you'd have to be a 20-ton Roman statue to keep your torso from moving with the pull. The main value of a belay device is that it requires very little strength to hold even the longest possible fall, and there's little chance of it ever failing, or the belayer suffering abrasions or rope burns—if the whole system is properly rigged. When the disparity of weight is substantial between belayer and leader, a belay device is certainly advisable. For two years I did most of my climbing with a woman whom I outweighed by

The Sticht plate

over one hundred pounds. I fell dozens of times, and she always caught me effortlessly, and never got a scratch. Here are a few of the most popular devices:

The first of the belay devices to appear was the Sticht Plate, invented by a German engineer in the early 1970s and still the most popular, though others are gaining fast. The plate is a 4-ounce disk with a channel hole machined through it. A bight of rope is passed through the channel and clipped through a locking carabiner in your harness or swami. (Two opposing gated regular biners will work, though not as well) The plate has a keeper loop which, when clipped into the carabiner, keeps the plate from floating out away from the waist. Since the plate will sometimes lock up when you don't want it to, some plates have a spring on the back to prohibit this. When belaying, the rope passes in, around the carabiner, and out through the plate again, your hands doing exactly what they would for a body belay. To hold a fall, the brake hand is pulled to the brake hand's side: The plate collapses on the biner and the rope is locked fast. As with all belay devices, make certain the live end of the rope emerges on the same side as the direction of pull: Don't get the ropes crossed. Sticht plates come in all manner of sizes and dimensions for use with 9, 10, and 11 millimeter rope, and other configurations for double ropes. There is a generic plate, but the later versions are for specific rope sizes.

Recently there have appeared micro versions of the Sticht plate which, though they work exactly like the Sticht, are as strong, and weigh less than one ounce, are oftentimes too small for 11 mm ropes, and usually overheat quickly.

The Lowe Tuber is a cone-shaped tube. A bight of rope passes in and around a locking carabiner and back out the tube. During a fall, the tube, rather than a plate, locks the rope off at the biner. The amount of working friction depends on what end of the tube you have against the locking biner. Like the Sticht plate, a keeper loop holds the tuber close to the biner. Popular and light.

The Lowe Tuber

Long used by stevedores to tether onerous loads on the docks, the Munter hitch is a handy alternative to devices, for it only requires a special carabiner attached to your harness or swami. When Swiss climber Werner Munter introduced this hitch to climbing—claiming the invention—the UIAA

The Munter hitch:

1. Twist rope
2. Twist again.
3. Clip doubled rope in,
4. and pull up and out.

conducted extensive tests, gave it thumbs up, and it's steadily caught on ever since. During the fall, the brake hand goes out, and the hitch locks on itself. Only use a "pearbiner"—an oversized pear-shaped biner with a locking gate—with the Munter hitch. The mouth on a regular, or even a D carabiner, is not wide enough to keep the hitch from binding when you don't want it to. Most climbers who have tried the Munter hitch stay with it. The action is good, the set-up instantaneous, and you don't have to carry a device, even if it only weighs an ounce. There is a tendency for the rope to get excessively kinked, however. And a word of caution: Since the rope is continually running through the biner, the action can unscrew the sleeve on a locking biner, so crank the sleeve tight before belaying, and keep an eye on it.

There are dozens of other devices, but they all involve either a knot locking on itself or around a device, or a bight of rope locked off by the device. While the devices take the doubt out of belaying for many smaller climbers, it's essential to learn the fundamentals with the body belay. If you change over to the devices, you know the basic method if you should drop or forget the device—which happens. The devices perform only as well as you know how to use them, and a good belay is safe only if you observe the rules we've laid down: The belay anchor must be inviolate; always tie in taut to the belay anchor; get in line with, and anticipate the direction of pull; maintain a good brace or stance; stay alert; and the golden rule—never take your brake hand off the rope, lest your belay prove lethal to your partner and, perhaps, to yourself.

Top-roping

TOP-ROPING

Remember to use doubled biners on the anchor!

Practice the skills you've learned so far on a short cliff first, anchoring at the top and belaying from below—top-roping. Many regular climbing areas have cliffs that are ideally suited to this fun activity. With a top rope you can gain climbing skills as well as practice catching simple falls without quite the seriousness of facing a big cliff. As we've discussed, be certain that the top anchor is a stout natural anchor like a tree, or put in at least two—better make it three—nuts or other artificial anchors. Equalize the load by running slings from each anchor to a common point, having the slings that connect it all droop just over the top of the cliff so the running rope won't bind. Clip the rope through two carabiners—gates opposed—and, until you gain experience to accurately judge potential loads, always be sure to tie the belayer into an anchor on the ground. Have fun!

The Art of Leading

Most veterans admit that climbing doesn't really start until you cast off on the lead. You can boulder around enchanted forests and follow a leader up the world's greatest rock climbs, but the moment you're the *first* on the rope, it's suddenly real in an altogether different way. Everything is magnified manyfold as now you're playing for keeps. The decisions are all yours—as are the rewards, and consequences. Whether that first lead is up a razor-cut crack at the base of El Capitan, or on some filthy slab in a scrap heap quarry, the feeling of command, and the special demands, are always the same. It's no longer just an exhilarating physical challenge, but a creative problem-solving design requiring a lot of intangible things and with the penalty of injury, or even death, for a major oversight.

Because leading is a procedure involving equipment and an applied system, we can nail down certain objective realities, at least in a generic sense. But the deeper we go, the greyer it all becomes. It's like discussing a fine painting or a classic wine: if you talk long enough, you'll be babbling regardless of your expertise. Every climb, like every canvas, every wine, is a little different, and very little applies to one and all. Every climber is ultimately self-taught. We can open the way a bit, suggesting what fine leading is about, and not about, and ever stressing safety, but more than that must not be expected from an instruction manual.

The First Lead

Ideally, you will have taken a climbing course and had the fundamentals drummed into you by a competent instructor. You will have spent time placing nuts, rigging and equalizing anchors, so when you grab the lead, you don't have nagging doubts about your ability to do the basic things safely. You will have complemented your practical experience by reading this manual, or one like it. And you will have served at least a brief apprenticeship following an experienced leader up a host of climbs, becoming familiar with the nuances which a book, or even the best personal instruction, cannot impart. And ideally I would be a Sultan on a South Pacific Island with no duties save to count my trunkful of black pearls. We don't live in an ideal world, and many first-time leaders have little experience. Some have no experience.

Others can't be bothered with instruction and don't want to follow anyone, anywhere. They'll lead from day one and thank you very much for your advice. I don't suggest this latter tactic. It's a quick way to get hurt. You don't want to learn leading through trial and error. A first time leader should know the whole procedure well before stepping out as boss. But either way, you'll have to decide what it is you want to lead.

Guidebooks

Picture a cliff, a quarter mile long and 300 feet high. Folks first started climbing there in 1950, and the cliff has become a favorite for sport climbers. Since the first climber discovered the first way up the cliff, exploration has been steady until now there are over 300 different ways—or "routes"—up the wall. How do we know this? Since 1950, each route was recorded and later published in a guidebook. A guidebook lists first ascents—the names and dates of the first people to climb a given route.

Each route is named and rated by the first ascenders and, by the time a route makes it into print, it's usually had enough ascents that the rating is fairly objective, arrived at by consensus. Most guidebooks have several master photos, with lines superimposed to show the various routes, or at least prominent features allowing one to find specific climbs by reference. A guidebook is indispensable—to experts, who want to know where the hardest routes are, and to beginners, who yearn for easy ground, and everyone in between. It allows us to pick a route that best suits our taste and expertise. Many guides have a quality rating, or at least a list of recommended routes; so a visiting climber can spend a few days and know he's tasted some of the best the crag has to offer. A guide is particularly important for the beginning leader, who can use all the guidance he can get.

Typical guidebook topo

The early guides used photos and written descriptions. In the mid seventies the written description was replaced by the "topo", or topographic guide. A topo is simply a minimal blueprint of the climb—really just a detailed line-drawing—featuring prominent features, belay locations, the type of climbing (liebacking, etc.), and the difficulty, all rendered in a facile set of symbols. This graphic representation of cliffs and their climbs is the most precise and convenient means of route description, easily understood and capable of crossing language barriers. Every topo guide has a key at the beginning to clarify the symbols, though most are obvious.

Topos are normally more detailed than the prose guides but are still in truncated form, so it takes some experience to learn how to read them at a glance. Though rare, some guides still use prose descriptions, so become familiar with both formats. Many times the guidebook is bulky, so climbers often xerox the topos and carry a page instead of a book.

Pick a route well within your abilities for that first lead. Most every cliff has a classic easy route which hundreds of people have broken in on. Whatever you choose, be certain the protection is sound, that you are at least somewhat adept in the techniques involved, and that the route is straightforward, requiring no unusual shenanigans or special skills. A direct, easy climb, that's what you want. If the first lead proves too easy, no one's stopping you from hopping right back onto something a little stiffer. Getting in over your head on your first lead is a horrible and potentially dangerous experience, and may color, if not end, your climbing career. Take it slow. Cut loose only when you know what's happening.

The Rack

The collection of gear the climber takes up the climb is called the rack. There are two considerations: what gear to take, and how to take, or "rack" it.

Once you have decided on a climb, the guidebook should tell you the requisite equipment needed for safe passage. If it doesn't, you're left to eyeball the route and estimate what's needed. A "standard" rack may be the catch-all rack that works for 80 percent of the routes at 80 percent of the areas. This consists of a complete set of "wires" —cabled micro tapers to tapers of about an inch across, a progressively sized selection of hexentrics or SLCDs to about two or three inches, five or six over-the-shoulder-length runners, carabiners for each nut carried, and a few extra as well. In any case, climbers routinely ask around to get the lowdown—what's the best rack, is there any hidden placement and where is it, and does a certain nut work best at the crux. One can waste considerable time getting such advice, which is sometimes contradictory because everyone does things a little differently. Also, the suggested rack is often a little "thin", so use your own judgement. The suggested rack normally refers only to sizes encountered, not spelling out the nuts by brand names. Learn to translate this relative to the gear you own. And remember: it's better to take more than you need than less.

There are two methods to rack gear, or "hardware": on a gear sling worn over the shoulder, or on gear loops on the side of your harness. It's give or take with both methods. On steep and overhanging climbs, gear on a shoulder sling will follow

Racking methods

Climbing Signals

"ON BELAY?" The question the climber asks before he proceeds.

"BELAY ON" The response the belayer tells the climber when his belay is set and ready.

"CLIMBING" What the climber says to the belayer indicating he—the climber—is starting to climb.

"CLIMB" The belayers response that he's ready to belay the rope, proceeding to do so as the climber advances.

"SLACK" A command to the belayer to let out some rope, give slack.

"UP ROPE" A command to the belayer to take in the rope, pull up the slack.

"TENSION" A command to the belayer to hold the climber on tension by holding the belay fast.

"WATCH ME" Commands the belayer to pay close attention, expect or be prepared for a fall.

"FALLING!" The climber is falling—a statement of fact.

"BELAY OFF" The climber's signal to the belayer that he has anchored himself and that the belayer's responsibility to belay should end.

"OFF BELAY!" The belayer's response to the climber that the belay has ended.

"ROCK!" Akin to yelling "Fore" on a golf course. Rocks are coming down; take cover.

"ROPE!" A rope is coming down; watch for it.

gravity and slip around your back, making quick access difficult. Gear racked on a harness hangs directly over both hips, and depending on your free hand, you may discover the desired nut on the opposite hip, requiring an awkward reach and some fumbling to even unclip it.

Whatever method you choose, gear should be racked systematically according to size, in an order you have memorized for ready access. Rack small nuts up front, progressively bigger going back. SLCDs and medium to large hexes are racked individually—one biner for each nut. Clip the carabiner in so the gate is facing the body and opens from the top. This way the thumb will naturally go to the gate and you can lift the nut straight off, rather than having to twist it about, opening the gate with your fingers. Wired nuts are racked in bunches, from micro-nuts on up, perhaps six on one biner. How they are clipped onto your rack depends on how you want them. Some climbers unclip the appropriate bunch, fit the nut of choice, unclip it from the bunch and return the remainder to the rack. Others know at first glance what nut they want and remove it individually from the sling or harness. (If you're wrong, it's better to have had the whole bunch in hand for an easy second try.) If you remove wires individually, rack the carabiner gate out, so you can lift the nut out, instead of back and under. If you remove the whole bunch, rack the biner so the gate faces your body. Free biners should be racked together, in front of, or behind the nuts. (Additional equipment will be explained later.)

Starting Out

You've picked a route and you know where it goes. You're racked up, tied in and breathing fire, but who's that tending your line? A cousin sprung from reform school to whom you explained the fundamentals on the hike in? No, sir! You must have full confidence that your belayer will catch you if you fall. If you can, get an experienced climber to belay you for that first lead. He can give valuable coaching from below, and can critique your lead once done. Moreover, you know he can belay, can catch any fall you'll take, which frees your mind to concentrate on the lead.

A standardized protocol of communication removes any doubt as to what the leader and the belayer are doing, are expected to do, are asked to do, and are warned to do. It is described at left. When you anticipate being unable to hear each other because of river noise, say, work out your own protocol in rope tugs *before* the leader starts the pitch. Maybe three sharp tugs from the leader would mean you can take him off belay and two sharp tugs from the leader means you can climb. In such difficult situations it is the resposibility of the belayer to be particularly sensitive to the rope so the climber has the proper amount of slack or tension.

Before you start up, study the rock above. Spot any key holds, obvious features, or nut placements. Climb up mentally, imagining the required techniques. On easy climbs, the seqence is usually no mystery—just a matter of execution, so picture yourself doing the moves, then go at it.

The first section above the ground is crucial because if you fall there, you hit the deck. So climb no higher than you feel comfortable jumping off from, then set your first nut. (All gear placed to protect the leader is called "protection", or simply "pro") Make certain that first pro is especially good. And make certain your belayer knows you're clipped in. To the first pro, the belay is worthless as you aren't clipped into anything. Now you're plugged in, and the system is operative. If the pro seems questionable, double it up—place two, or even three nuts until you know something will stop your fall. At the outset, the leader must always calculate how far he has to fall to hit the ground, and he should always have some pro in to preclude this. Up higher, once you have several nuts in—providing they're good—"decking out" is no longer a concern. But "rope drag" is.

Protection: The Direction of Pull

As a leader, you must continually assess the direction the rope will pull on all the protection below you, should you fall. Until you can, you won't be a safe leader. Though it sounds confusing, the concept is easy:

Rarely does a climb follow a perfectly straight line. Even cracks curve and snake around, so the rope to some extent has to bend about according to the contour of the crack your pro is in. To ably predict the direction of pull, a leader must be conscious of the various forces on *the entire system*. When you fall, the rope comes tight and the transmission of force pulls all the protection toward the middle, toward an imaginary straight line between leader and belayer. Pro not placed directly in that line is subject to considerable sideways and upward pull, and can easily be wrenched free if you have not compensated for the oblique force. So when the route zigzags around, there are certain things we do.

You always want the rope to follow as straight a line as possible, even if all your protection is from bolts (which cannot be wrenched free from sideways forces). The more crooks the rope makes, the greater the friction—the "rope

(top): Stressing a cara-biner sideways over an edge is weak and wrong.

(bottom): Much better is to use a longer sling.

(top) Incorrect use of a nut sling as a runner, and (bottom) the much stronger way.

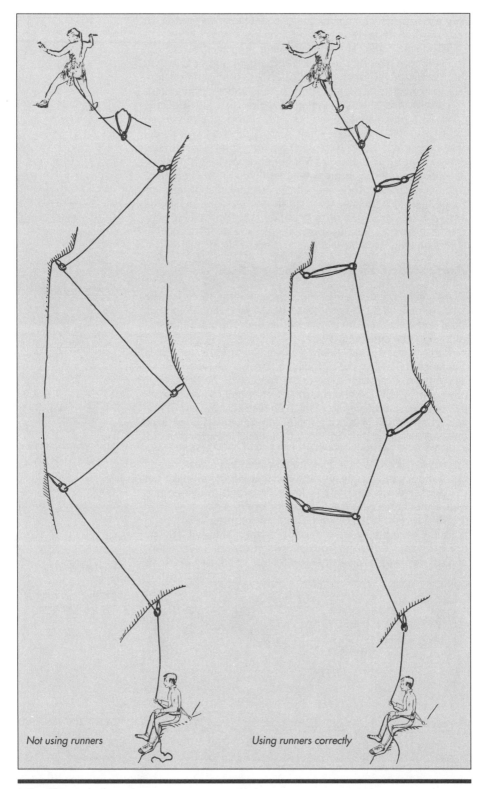

Not using runners

Using runners correctly

drag"—which in degrees, is like the belayer holding you back. An experienced leader imagines a plumb-line between the belayer and the end of the first pitch, and arranges protection so the rope follows that line as closely as possible. When protection is by necessity placed to the side of the plumb-line, we attach runners to the pro which, in effect, extends the rope toward the imaginary line. The drawback with runners is that they increase the potential fall twice the length of the runner. For this reason, and because the runner is like a free tether and can move, rather than being just a fixed point, it is very rare that someone will attach a runner bigger than the normal length worn over the shoulder. If the runner is well off to the side, and a fall will still transmit lateral force on the nut, either set the nut with a firm downward jerk, or place an oppositional nut beneath it to form a multi-directional protection. The theory is simple: You are not just trailing a rope, but dragging it through your protection. Runners keep that drag at a minimum, and keep the nuts in place.

Use of a multi-directional anchor to prevent the rope from lifting the protection from the crack.

When clipping into fixed protection or cabled nuts, even if they're placed in a direct line, it's advisable to use quickdraws. Quick-draws are small, sewn runners, fashioned from either 1", or 9/16" tubular webbing and harbor two carabiners, one for the pro, one for the rope. Quick-draws are short, so they don't appreciably increase the potential fall, and they really facilitate the rope running smoothly. Moreover, cabled nuts are stiff, and when clipped off with single, or even double biners, can be lifted from the crack by rope drag. Quick-draws prevent this. Some climbers prefer to rack their shoulder slings as quick-draws by tripling

(page opposite)

Using slings to allow the rope to run freely and keep the protection properly aligned.

QUICK-DRAWS
Shoulder length tripled
Sewn sling

Clipping into wired nuts:
(top to bottom)

Never thread sling mate-
rial directly into a wire;
with a solid fall the wire
will slice right on
through!

Never clip into an
anchor that has any stiffness to it (like a wire)
with two carabiners; a
twist in the rope can pull
the nut free or force the
biners to unclip them-
selves.

Correct use of the quick-
draw, with rope-end
biner gate down and out
to easily accept the rope.

the loops; this allows one to easily extend the quick-draws to
a full-sized runner as required.

As you climb, try to avoid having the rope run directly
between your legs—better is to trail it over a leg; in the
event of a fall there is then less danger of the tightening
rope flipping you over backwards and increasing chance of
head injury.

When to Place Protection

There is no hard and fast rule concerning when to place
protection or when to simply carry on. Experienced climbers
place pro when they need it. To the beginning leader the
experience is all new and he might not know when he needs
pro; he is likely to think he always needs it. You definitely
want sound protection at the start of a pitch, and before any
hard, or "crux" section. Anticipate the crux; place protection
when you can, not to count on the fact that you can slot
something fifteen feet higher at the hard move. Whenever
you encounter an obvious bottleneck or are resting on a big
hold, slot a nut no matter how easy the climbing is. If the
climbing feels manageable and you feel good, go ten or fifteen feet between nuts and feel the thrill and freedom of the

lead. But always be aware of ledges or features you may hit should you fall, and protect yourself accordingly. Avoid the temptation to "run the rope out", going long distances between protection, even if the climbing is clearly easy. Once you are a good judge of both your own prowess and the terrain encountered, do whatever you like. But the beginning leader will rarely want to go more than about fifteen feet between nuts. That's only eight nuts for a 120-foot pitch, which isn't excessive by any count.

If one hand is holding you to the rock, clipping in can be trying. The universal method is: Reach down below your tie-in, pull up a loop and hold it in your teeth. Reach down for more slack, then clip in. Sounds odd, but there's not a leader alive who doesn't do this. Sometimes fixed protection is found in awkward positions and can be very strenuous to even clip. Climbers sometimes rig quick-draws with one end clipped to a shoulder sling, the other clipped through the lead rope. At a desperate clip, just unclip from the gear sling and clip the fixed pro and your rope is clipped in as well. If you discover the fixed pro is good enough, you're set. If it's bad, you're no worse off.

Bent-gate carabiners, though great to clip a rope into, should only be used for that purpose. Don't use them to clip into a bolt, fixed pin, or wired nut. Even quickdraws can bind and open the gate all too easily. Watch them.

Using two wires woven together to reach a good placement.

Rope clenched in gritted teeth, Todd Skinner grapples to clip a bolt on the muscular "Calling All the Heroes" (5.13d), Hueco Tanks, Texas. Extremely strenuous climbs like this are the domain of the world-class cragsman, and few hear the call to tackle such leads. In the case of "Calling All the Heroes", few are heroes; most fail.

Bill Hatcher photo

Route Finding

Part of learning to be a good leader is knowing what makes a bad one—knowing how climbers defeat themselves—and avoiding these needless mistakes. Good climbing requires you to use available holds the easiest way; good routefinding requires you to keep to the easiest holds. Follow the line of least resistance, not wandering onto more difficult rock on the flanks. Route finding is part instinct, part experience (which you might not be long on). Study the topo and compare it against what you see. Locate salient features, like bushes or roofs, and know where the hard parts are in relation to them. The topo should tell you this information—i.e., that the section above the bush is hard, that the crux is after the crack peters out. Get yourself prepared *before* you start by memorizing all the given information.

If you feel you have wandered off the route, look for the signs: Chalk marks, boot marks, fixed protection, broken flakes or holds. On popular routes, the texture and color of the rock is often different, smoother and lighter than bordering stone, because hundreds of boots have paddled over every hold, probably for many years. With crack climbs, the route is often obvious. Face climbs are more nebulous.

Cruxes: The Hard Parts

Even easy climbs have cruxes, sections harder than the rest. You will recognize them because the holds will suddenly run out, the crack will thin, widen, get shallow, or the angle will bulge. Don't climb mechanically, but with all your savvy. Recognize the crux before you are on it. Set a good nut, or several nuts. Study the holds or crack and plot a likely strategy; but once you have committed yourself to it, improvise if your theory is wrong and climb aggressively. Use whatever works best, and easiest, which sometimes is an improbable sequence. If a fall seems possible, or likely, make certain your pro is adequate, and observe what, if anything, you will hit if you come off. If everything checks out, alert your belayer and go after it. No leader wants to fall, and you don't start up something without some hope of succeeding. The fact that success is not a given defines the challenge in climbing. But the fear of falling prohibits one's best effort and if everything checks out the fears are groundless. Falling is part of sport climbing. Good protection and realistic judgement keeps the sport sane.

Falling

Fifty years ago the incontrovertible rule was: The leader must *never* fall. The equipment was unreliable, and there was always the chance of the rope breaking. Present day gear is remarkably sound, and while no one wants to fall, controlled falling has become standard practice for virtually all active sport climbers. Many leading climbers don't feel they have

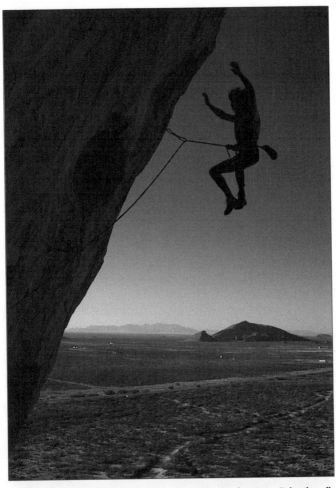

Bracing for impact, Labuddy Willoughby whistles off "Old Legends Die" (5.13b), Hueco Tanks, Texas. Note how Labuddy maintains body control, which greatly minimizes potential injury. Labuddy was unscathed and later completed the climb.

Beth Wald photo

pushed themselves until they have logged some "air time". Indeed, you can never discover your limits unless you exceed them. Climbers routinely do and the smart ones rarely get a scratch, even from twenty-foot falls. This relaxed attitude is not due entirely to the gear, however. Climbers have become expert in calculating the risks and potential consequences, and people have learned how to fall.

There are only two issues involved when you commit yourself to a potential fall: is the protection adequate to hold the longest possible fall, and what will you hit should you fall. The belay is never in question because you simply don't climb with someone who can't hold your fall unless you're a lunatic. If the pro is sound and the rock steep and smooth, it's fairly common to see a climber spend a whole afternoon falling off a difficult route. However, if the protection is dubious and there's something to hit, it's very rare to see a climber carry on unless he is virtually certain he will not fall. It's not the act of falling, but the consequences which are the issue. Climbing and protecting are separate skills, each of which keeps you alive, so for any lead—especially the first—don't challenge yourself in both at the same time. The beginning leader should avoid falling at all costs, but the possibility will arise and both his and the expert's concerns are the same: the security of the pro, and what he might hit if he loses it.

Falling is an art. When you fall, you need to maintain body control, to stay facing the rock, and to avoid tumbling. On a slab, you slide down on your feet, both hands pressing off the slab, keeping your chest and head far away from the surface. Keep your legs bent and spread apart, cat-like. The

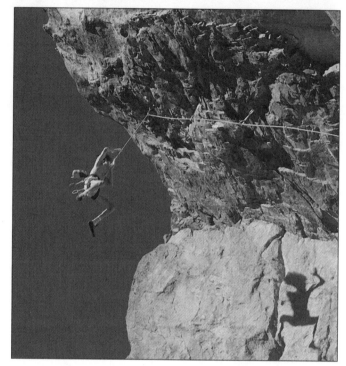

Sayonara! Chasing his fleeting shadow, Hidataka Suzuki sails off the lip of the extremely overhanging "Your Mamma" (5.12c/d), in Eldorado Canyon, Colorado. However daunting, the climber was held fast and he grazed nothing but mountain air in a fall routine to experts.

Bob Horan photo

rope stretches considerably, so the jolt is less than you might think. I caught a partner on a fifty-footer on a steep slab which did nothing but wear his boots out prematurely. He stayed relaxed, and just slid down on his feet, balancing with his hands—like a high angle slide. I saw another person take the same fall, freeze up, and start tumbling. He needlessly broke a wrist.

On vertical climbs, you don't slide, but plummet—and very quickly. Remember to keep your legs a little extended and bent, so at impact they absorb the force like shock absorbers. Don't freeze up or go limp. That only invites injury. The screaming, rag-doll fall is worse still. The flailing arms will invariably smack something.

When you have traversed away from protection, a fall will swing you, pendulum fashion. The cat-like stance is your only hope to avoid tumbling. Be prepared for your weight coming onto the rope, which otherwise can wrench you askew, even spin you like a top. Remember, pendulum falls are dangerous no matter your posture or agility. Slamming into a corner from twenty feet to the side is little less than falling twenty feet straight down and smacking a ledge on your side.

Even a long fall happens so fast that you don't have time to think. All the stories about a person's life flashing before his eyes are pure bunk. You only have time to react. Often it's the shorter, eight to 10-foot falls which are the real wrenchers, where little rope is out, and the rope stretches less than on a longer fall. But whatever the length, don't freeze up, stay relaxed, facing the wall, legs and arms bent, and you'll usually not be hurt *if* your calculations were right.

After a fall of more than 20 feet, the rope suffers appreciable fiber elongation and structural deformation, much of which is recovered in time. After a longish fall, lower down and wait at least ten minutes for the rope to recover some of it's stretch. The knot will absorb up to 30 percent of the impact force, so after lowering down, tie into your anchor with a sling, untie the knot, then retie it after your rest.

Often you will know you're going to fall before you do: you're bunched up and can't move; your fingers or toes are buttering off the holds; or your strength is ebbing fast. Warn your belayer, and don't panic. Fall as gracefully as you can. Not to impress anyone, but to keep your form. The person who falls out of control may have popped unexpectedly but more likely panicked once airborne—a sure recipe for trouble. Don't underestimate even the smallest fall. A fall can break bones and even kill you if it goes wrong, so calculating and reacting to the consequences is extremely important. This is something a manual can only suggest.

Loose Rock

Most climbs of any length have at least some loose or rotten rock and the two are quite different, though the dangers are real in both cases. Loose rock doesn't necessarily mean the rock quality is poor. A flake, chockstone, block, or hold might be diamond hard but still ready to go if you so much as breathe on it. Common sense is your best guide here. Delicately test suspect holds (if you have to use them) by tapping them with the heel of your hand. The sound can tell you a lot. Try and avoid them if at all possible. Arrange your protection so the rope goes around them. If there is a chance of them coming off, warn your belayer.

Rotten rock, crumbly and decomposing, is a nightmare. Every hold, every flake, every nut is suspect because you simply don't know what will hold and what won't. It's all instinct and judgement. Stay clear of such routes until you have the experience to know you shouldn't climb them anyway. If you dislodge rocks onto the rope, inspect the whole rope at the first opportunity. A bounding stone can chop even a new rope in a heartbeat.

*It is the leader's respon-
sibility to ensure that
the second does not
have to follow a crux
traverse without protec-
tion, usually simply a
matter of putting in pro
AFTER the crux.*

Protecting the Second

The leader is responsible for the second's well being as well as his own. He's got to do more than just warn the belayer of rock fall, or tell him he's about to fall. He must protect the second with the same acumen as he protects himself. This is most essential on traverses, where the leader moves sideways off a piece of protection. Note that when the leader reaches a traverse, he slots a nut which protects him going sideways. When the second follows, he cleans that nut and if he falls off, he'll swing all the way to the next nut. When the rope runs dead horizontal, it's very hard to keep from tumbling if you fall, so a leader should always protect at regular intervals—for his, and his partners safety.

Leading on the Face

Aside from what's already been said, it's a slippery task trying to explain the alchemy of leading a difficult face climb. Still, maybe this will help:

A good face climber is a master of strategy. The first step is to break the climb down to sections between obvious footholds or rest stops. That way you can concentrate on one section at a time. Before a crux section, arrange pro you are certain is sound so you can concentrate on the moves, not the consquences. Get on a foothold and scrutinize the face. Spot the best holds, break the section down to body lengths. Keep reducing each section down to the last visible hold. Then construct a mental sequence and visualize yourself climbing it. If it's too strenuous to pause very long, size up the holds, and cast off. On strenuous leads, you have to be aggressive and really go after it; but never abandon your form. Look at the baseball player who goes with the grand slam swing. Instead of trying to stroke the ball, he tries to murder it. He's overanxious, and usually returns to the pine under a hail of boos. Savvy, alertness, and controlled aggression are all vague terms that apply to leading a hard face.

Learning to downclimb is a particularly important skill to the face climber. If you know you can reverse a section, than you minimize the potential danger and fear. Successful leaders will often venture out several times to gain the confidence to eventually go for it, gaining familiarity with each effort, and further reducing the hard section to the last, crux move. Hard face climbs are often not reversible, and eventually you will have to go for it, anyway. But climbing up and down can often help a leader settle in and muster the needed resolve.

Leading Crack Climbs

We have discussed the requisite techniques for climbing cracks but the fact is, often the hardest part of leading a crack is not the climbing, but arranging the protection. When the climbing is strenuous, the leader finds himself hanging from a questionable jam and desperately trying to place a nut. Here are a few tricks to remember:

On thin to medium-sized cracks, don't plug up the best jams with protection. A good leader will often opt for a smaller nut which fits into constrictions between the bigger, better jams.

You will normally place protection above your hands. Sometimes, if the only good nut slots are where your fingers are, you will place a nut below your hands, slotting it just after you have removed your fingers. Try and set these nuts quickly, as often you are hanging on in a crunched-up position, with a bent arm, which is more strenuous than the straight arm hang.

Be conscious that your feet don't get entangled in the rope. If your foot gets caught under both the rope and the nut, an upward step can lift your nut from the crack.

When the crack is parallel-sided and strenuous, go with SLCD's, which are much faster to place, and usually better.

Utilize all rest opportunities, and get a good nut in while you're there. Arrange sound protection before any crux section of liebacking or jamming, and if it's safe, power over the section without stopping. Hanging on in the middle of a crux section to get added protection in is often the wrong tactic, and can result in a fall you wouldn't have taken if you'd carried on.

Husband your energy. Don't use brute strength unless you need to. Stay relaxed, and try and get into a rhythm, a groove. Never thrash.

Setting the Belay

Once you have completed the first lead, you must rig an anchor to belay the second man up. The anchor, of course, must be atomic bombproof unless you wish to risk getting ripped off the wall if the second falls. There are countless different possible belay constructs, all dictated by what the climb affords. As mentioned, always stop at an obvious ledge or belay spot. Try and rig the anchor directly above the line of ascent, so you can belay in-line with the direction of pull. If you're on a ledge, tie yourself off with enough slack so you can belay at the lip of the ledge. This facilitates easy rope handling and communication, and keeps the rope from running over a potentially sharp edge. You'll usually choose to sit, facing out and down but you can stand if you have a good brace. Just make certain you are tied off taut to the belay. If not, a fall could drag you right over the lip. Not good.

If the belay is on a small ledge or stance, you'll belay facing the anchor. Tie in with enough slack so you can lean back.

Rig the rope so it comes up, runs through the anchor, then back to you. Belaying through the anchor puts the load directly on the hardware so (for the hundredth time) the anchor must be stout. Also, the force of a fall will draw you directly toward the wall, so remained braced.

Belaying through the anchor is not a requirement. Climbers do so as it is usually safer and always more comfortable. The anchor, rather than you waist, takes the bulk of the force during a fall. If for some reason you cannot get an anchor to your utmost satisfaction—which does happen—you should probably belay right off your waist. When the second man falls, the force is not extreme, and if you're properly braced and ready, your torso can absorb the force, often with no help from the anchor at all.

Some climbers argue that you should never belay through the anchor because it loads the system unnecessarily. They would rather the torso absorb at least some of the force, saving the anchor for a backup. But for me and thousands of others the anchor is not a back up but the whole shooting match, and all the talk about saving, or guarding the anchor is balderdash. Anyone who has climbed a big wall knows that if your anchor isn't good enough to belay through, it's not an anchor at all, but a lethal liability.

Sometimes there are no belay ledges, or stances, or even good footholds. Here you must construct a "sling", or "hanging" belay. Many hanging belays feature permanent anchors—bolts, pitons, or both. If you have to construct an artificial anchor, observe the rules we've gone over. Once the anchor is all equalized, tie yourself off with enough slack so you can hang at, but not below the hardware—and not so far out that you can't easily reach the anchor if need be. You

(photo opposite)

A HANGING BELAY

1. Nuts held in opposition by clove hitches tied into a sling.

2. A clove hitch in the rope ties the first anchor set in opposition to a series of downward-pull nuts and also connects to

3. A main figure-eight tie-in for the belayer. Note that this all leaves her a bit below the upward-pull nuts, not the ideal situation, but certainly acceptable since any upward movement forced by a leader fall would be soon checked by the nuts.

4. Hanging her weight on the anchors is only practical at this small station and adds counterweight security to the belay.

5. The leader has wisely run the rope through a good downward-pull anchor at the belay to direct the impact force away from directly on the belayer's waist.

6. The extra rope has been carefully lap-coiled across a sling to prevent it being caught by the wind or a flake below.

normally belay through the anchor on a hanging belay.

If you're wearing neither leg loops or a harness, you should carry a belay seat ("butt-bag") to sit in. Hanging off a swami is uncomfortable and rough on your back and kidneys. If you don't have a belay seat, create a loop of rope to sit on by tying the free rope back under your butt and to the anchor. Anything but hanging directly off your back.

Whatever construct you end up in, always pay close attention to the rope. As you belay it in, keep it organized: Stack it neatly. Don't let it loop down onto the rock below unless it can't get in the second's way, and there are absolutely no knobs or flakes for it to snag on. Never flip the slack into a deep crevice or behind a narrow flake. If there's anything for it to snag on, it will. If need be, loop the slack over your lap (lap-coiling), or through a sling, thus keeping it out of potential snares. This is essential with sea-cliff climbing.

If you climb long enough, you'll probably lose a rope due to a hang up, even if you're paying close attention. Strong winds, common on north faces, can blow the unattended rope exactly where you don't want it.

Changing Leads

Once the second has followed the pitch, having cleaned all the protection you put in, the first thing he does upon gaining the belay is to tie himself off—*before* he is taken off belay. And he should tie into more than one biner. Pull out the topo. Eyeball the hell out of the next lead and re-rack the gear accordingly. Don't take off with an unorganized rack because you won't want to fumble with the gear in an awkward position above. Relax. And don't take off until you have gone through the ceremony of figuring out as much as you can from below. Discuss questions and strategy with your partner. All this can take only a few minutes once you get the hang of it.

Though your anchor is bomb proof, there's no need to prove it is, so get a few nuts in *immediately* off the belay. Falling directly onto the belay is a worst case scenario. With a hip belay it is misery and possible disaster. The belay devices will do the job, but the force can sprain backs and slam the belayer into the wall hard enough to knock him cold. Even a short fall onto the belay transmits to both belayer and the anchor forces in excess of a thousand pounds and there is always the chance you might land on the belayer, somehow jarring his brake hand free, in which case, you'll plummet to the end of the rope, or the ground, whichever comes first. So even if the climbing is simple, get some pro in straightaway. To do otherwise is to violate a rule as fundamental as never removing your brake hand from the belay rope.

If you are not "swinging leads", and the second intends to follow every pitch, you face several options depending on the nature of the belay station. If you're on a good ledge, you can both tie into the anchor with slings looped through your

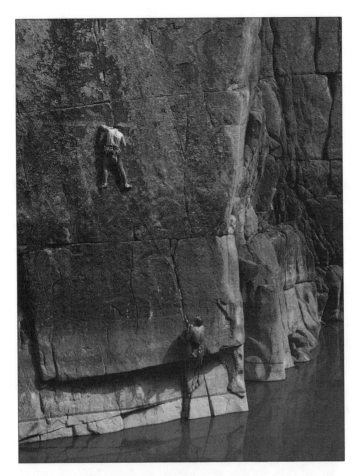

harnesses. The leader unties from the anchor and ties the
second in as he was tied in. That gives the leader a free rope,
and he's set to go. On small stances or hanging belays this
can be an enormous hassle, and you will often choose to simply change ends—untying your knots, and swapping ends.
Remember that you will at least briefly be untied from the
rope, so make certain that your sling tie-ins are secure, and
fastened with at least two biners to an equalized point.

If you are a party of three, it is easiest for the third
climber to climb last on a second rope that is trailed by the
second climber. At the belay, the third is tied off, and the free
end is trailed again on the following lead. If the third climber
wishes to lead a pitch, he simply is put on belay, clipped
through the anchor, and off he goes. If for some reason he
wants to go second, you are looking at some weird rope
shenanigans, untying and knot switching, which is more hassle than it's worth but possible using the aforesaid techniques. If the route wanders, it is the second's job to clip the
third's rope through key nuts to check any drastic sideways
falls. The third climber must then remove the pro his rope
has been clipped through.

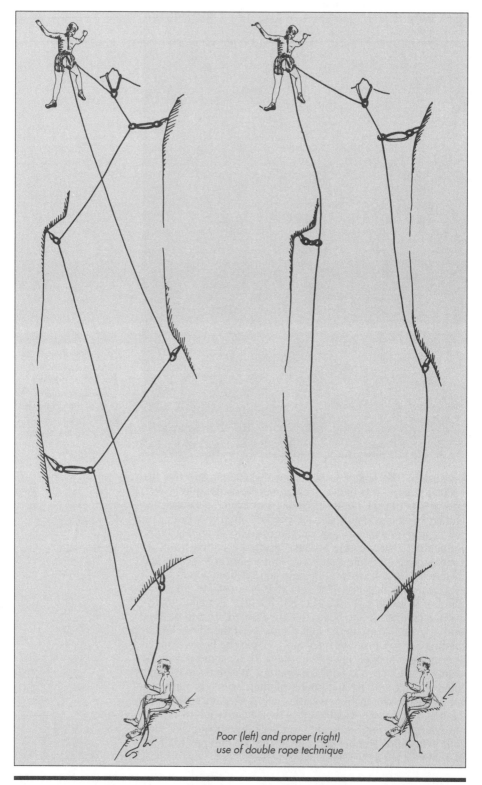

Poor (left) and proper (right)
use of double rope technique

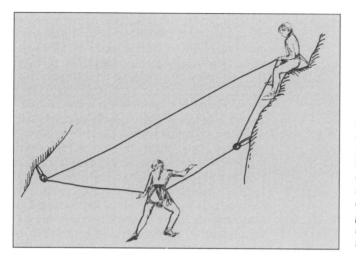

Protecting the second on a traverse with double ropes by belaying from both sides. The far anchor, remaining fixed, need only be as good as a sling through a fixed pin to secure the relatively gentle force of the falling second.

Double Rope Technique

Most Europeans and many British climbers lead on two 9mm ropes. For several reasons, the technique has never fully caught on in America. Managing a single 11mm lead rope is easier. There is less weight for the leader to drag behind him, and the belayers task is easier as well. Since American climbs tend to follow straight lines, the single 11mm rope has remained the standard. The advantages of using double ropes are these:

1) When a route wanders, a single rope will zig-zag extravagantly through the protection and a hundred runners can't eliminate rope drag. By using two different colored 9mm ropes, you can clip one line through protection on the left, and one on the right, each rope running somewhat parallel and straight—or at least avoiding the drastic jags of a single rope. 2) When the climber leading on a single rope pulls up a loop to clip in, he's adding distance to a potential fall at twice the length of the pulled-up loop. With double ropes, if the top pro should fail, or if he falls just before clipping in, the extra loop is not added to the fall since the other line is clipped in below, and he will come onto it first. 3) When the protection is poor, you can stack or duplicate placements, distributing the force of a fall between two nuts and two ropes, reducing impact on both. 4) On horizontal traverses, a single rope must go sideways with the line of protection. Providing that the leader was able to climb above the traverse before belaying, one of the double ropes can be left unclipped from the traverse protection, so the rope runs up and across to the belayer, instead of dead horizontal—much

Whenever two ropes are run through one anchor they should be clipped into separate carabiners.

Twin rope technique

better if the second should fall. 5) Perhaps the most important advantage is for those who climb regularly on sharp-edged rock like limestone, quartzite, or gneiss, where it is possible that a single rope could be cut during a fall. I've only heard once of a fall that resulted in a severed rope, but for those climbers frequenting areas where it is even conceivable, double ropes are a solution.

As the leader places pro, he will forewarn the belayer which rope he is going to clip in: "Slack on the yellow", for example. And herein lies the single biggest disadvantage with double ropes: their great potential for snarling and snagging—not only on rock features, but on themselves. A hip belay with double ropes is tricky business, requiring the lines to be fed out, or drawn in, alternately. With the belay devices, it's often hard to keep both lines running smoothly and ordered in a tidy pile. The lines can likewise become crossed in or behind the device. These problems are manageable with experience, so make sure you have some before belaying on double lines.

Twin Ropes

A recent technique involves leading on two 8.8mm ropes, using them as one rope, clipping *both* lines into the protection, though through separate biners. Aside from reducing the chance of total rope failure through cutting over an edge, there seems little else to recommend using twin ropes. A single strand of 8.8mm rope does not pass the regular UIAA test. It does pass the "half-rope" test, which substitutes a 50kg dropped weight for one weighing 80kg. Because it holds 7 such falls, climbers have started using the 8.8mm lines for double rope technique as well. With either twin or double ropes, it is safe practice to clip the first couple anchors off the belay with both ropes to safeguard against the high impact force of the leader falling close to the belay. With the thiner twin ropes this practice should be continued until well into the lead to provide plenty of rope to absorb any fall.

Twin rope technique, and using 8.8mm ropes as double ropes, are as yet unestablished practices, used only by experts in specialized situations. Time will render the verdict. For the novice, it's best to stick with the older, less complicated methods.

Retreat and Self Rescue

No climber has a 100 percent success ratio. Unexpected dangers, sore hands, hornets, apathy, no water, rain storms—the causes are many that may force a team off the cliff. There are two considerations when retreating: getting down unscathed, and doing so without leaving all your gear behind.

The most common practice is to simply lower the leader down to the belay. Oftentimes, if the leader doesn't fancy the pitch, the second will try his hand before the team throws the towel in altogether. If the decision is made to retreat, you will lower down, removing all the protection between the lowering point and the belay. This means that if what you are lowering off should fail, you will fall a very long way, so make certain whatever you lower off is bombproof. A good rule is to never lower off one nut. Back it up and equalize it, if necessary. And don't try and save a biner by running the rope through a runner threaded through the lower-off anchor. The generated friction on weighted nylon can saw right through it. Better to loose a piece of gear than your life. Dozens of climbers have thought otherwise, and paid dearly.

If the leader has more than half the rope out, he cannot return to the belay straight off because the rope won't reach. (Clearly, if you're 90 feet above the belay, you need 180 feet of rope to lower back to it, and the longest ropes are 165 feet.) He can either down climb to a point where he has sufficient rope to lower off, or he can lower down past the half way point—taking pro out as he descends and do this: arrange an anchor that is bombproof, and tie off to it with slings threaded through the harness or swami. Before you untie and pull the rope through, tie the rope off. You don't want it getting away from you, which would leave you marooned. Once you've pulled it through the top anchor, tie back in, take up the slack, and lower back down.

If the leader is hurt, or unconscious, you as belayer should try to lower him down, hopefully to a ledge. If there is not enough rope, you have little option but to tie him off, a procedure that may require innovation and the use of a prussik or Bachmann knot (discussed in the next chapter) in order to free yourself from the belay, then retreat for help (providing you have another rope)—or yell for it. And fast. An injured climber should not be left dangling. It constricts circulation, inhibits breathing, and his head will invariably be drooping in an abnormal attitude. Such a scenario is a true emergency and should be treated as one. A rescue team will have to climb up to him, establish an anchor, and lower him off on another free rope or come down from the top, whichever is easier. Such a procedure requires at least one other climber and two more ropes. So you'll need help, no matter who you are. The chief concern is to get the injured climber down quickly. It's usually much faster to simply leave all the gear behind, retrieving it when someone's health is not at stake.

If you are on exceptionally steep rock and left dangling from the wall after a fall, you should have foreseen the possibility. The belayer is left to tie you off. Wise leaders take another rope to pull back in with, or lead on double ropes for the same purpose. If you are on a single rope, you can often initiate enough swing—by flopping about in space—to pendulum back to the wall. If you can't, you're in a fine mess, and extracting yourself is quite involved. Hopefully there is some lesser angled rock below you can lower down to. If not, these are your options: try to hand over hand the rope back to the last nut, having the belayer reel the slack in once you've clasped the nut. This is nearly impossible, but it has been done. You can use a prusik or Bachmann knot setup to climb back up to the last nut (explained in chapter 6), or you can wait for a rescue. Someone will have to climb up to you, toss you a rope, and pull you back into the wall. If any of these scenarios are even remotely possible, you trail another rope so you can get back to the cliff. Anyone who doesn't almost deserves the consequent hassles.

There is another method of retreat involving rapelling off an anchor that we will discuss in the next chapter.

By predicting the possibilities you can avoid the consequences. You can never predict a rain storm or a case of the "willies", so expect at some time to "bail off" a climb. Just never bail off one nut, or lower down with your rope running through slings.

The Fear of Leading

Justified fear is a shrewd advisor, but groundless fear is self-defeating and can exhaust you. If you are terrified, quickly take stock of your situation. Is the belay good? It better be. That's a given. Is the protection adequate? If so, you might be confusing exhilaration with fear—which is common to beginners. Get on a foot hold and settle down. Relax. If you know you're safe yet still feel like fouling your britches, write it off to the jitters. If you eventually learn that you just can't adjust to the vertical environment, you might be in the wrong sport. Climbing's not for everyone.

Relaxation is essential in any exacting work. While telling someone to just relax is simple enough, beginning leaders often say, "Here I am, 100 feet up a vertical cliff, trembling on a little foothold with my rope clipped through a few pieces of wire. *How* am I supposed to relax?!" First, avoid things which cause a leader to panic. Never rush. Loss of concentration leads to poor self control and frantic climbing. Try to climb in a measured, self-contained manner. You're not in a race. Be realistic about the difficulties and hazards. If you're nervous, ask yourself why. Assess the problems. If the risks are imagined, you can usually talk yourself down. If they are real, you must retain self control. If you don't, you short circuit any rational response, and you might get hurt as a direct result of being afraid to get hurt.

The Psychology of Success

Climbers have long recognized the link between mental attitude and physical performance, and there's a lot of talk bandied about concerning visualization, imaging, zen breathing, et al. These disciplines can greatly magnify one's performance, but remember this: they're all ineffective if you can't unleash the tiger in your heart; and that's something that just can't be taught or acquired. Likewise, your mental attitude reflects your physical capabilities, and there are times that, even with the heart of a tiger, you still can't chin yourself on a burnished limestone wart, and there's no sense in telling yourself you can. The value of the mental exercises is to amplify your actual capabilities and to keep your mind from thwarting your full potential.

The important breakthroughs in climbing have not occurred because someone came along with stronger fingers and better boots. They occurred because someone had a new idea about what was possible, believed in himself, and had the fortitude to see it through. It all started with an idea, a belief.

The starting point to successful climbing is a positive attitude, an honest belief that you are going to give it your best shot, and that you have a chance at succeeding if all goes well. You cannot talk yourself into doing something you don't really want to do, or know you don't have a Chinaman's chance at. A positive attitude can bolster your resolve, but not create it. So on the day of an important climb, on the drive up to the cliff, while hiking to the base, we start programing our mind, telling ourselves that we can do what we set out to do if we believe it. We nip fear in the bud.

The next phase is to reduce our thoughts to the task at hand, eliminating extraneous ideas, emotions, small talk, distraction. Switch off the ghetto blaster and focus on the climb. Get relaxed. Concentrate. The mind is capable of doing many things at once, but only one well. Don't split your attention or derail it with things which won't further your immediate aim.

Before and during the climb, visualize yourself doing the moves, climbing smoothly and in complete control. The word "imaging" is popular just now, but it's the same old thing—and very effective: the basketball player visualizing the ball piercing the hoop with the game-winning shot, the climber seeing himself liebacking over the crux bulge. A climber might study the crux and preview several different sequences in his mind before the most probable one clicks a mental light on.

Throughout the whole process you are verbally telling yourself—silently and out loud—that you will succeed. This is no more than self hypnosis, auto suggestion, and can have remarkable impact on the receptive mind. When effectively done, you are programing the sub-conscious, where much of the reservations originate.

The ultimate performer is the one who climbs "unconscious". Not like a zombie, but one whose conscious, rational mind is not continually checking the upward flow with negative thoughts, and is only a distant observer. It's a trance-like state that only recognizes the task at hand. The will is crystallized, the attention needled down to a tiny section of space and time and when you get there the only thing that can hold you back is a true physical impossibility.

Some climbers are so keen to succeed that they defeat themselves by trying too hard. To these climbers, the mental disciplines are particularly effective, for they can instill the control and discipline that their natural gusto would have otherwise negated. The old notion that "the tiger hunts in absolute peace" best illustrates this point.

On the exceptionally difficult crux, all the mental games must conclude before you start. The most difficult climbs require a tenacity and degree of effort almost unheard of in any other sport. The mental games are remarkably effective as a beginning ritual but once you swing into that double overhanging lieback, or onto that bald and bulging face, it's no time to be talking to yourself or imagining anything. It's all focused effort.

A realistic goal; a strong desire; correct programing through visualization; verbal and non-verbal self-commands; and the focus, control, and tenacity to execute the task—that's what you're after.

Climbing with Style

That the fashion in which we go about climbing rocks is of any consequence to anyone is, on the face of it, debatable. We just want to get up safely, and if we ignore decorum here and there, who cares? But a funny thing happens once we are even moderately skilled. Simply getting up at all costs is not very satisfying. We slowly realize that the *way* we get up is both the means and the end. Anyone who sticks with climbing—virtually to the man—comes to this conclusion. To understand current mores, lets look at where they originated.

In the classic *Ropes, Knots, and Slings for Climbers,* Walt Wheelock talks about the "Golden Age" of climbing, centered in and around Zermatt, a century ago. "A rope was only to be used as a belay, not as a climbing aid. One just did not put his weight on the rope if he were a worthy member of the Alpine Club. It could be used to aid a descent and in the case of emergency or for safety, but each climber was expected to climb his own peak."

This "fair play" trend continued until climbers, in their search for new and harder routes, began using equipment for direct assistance. First were pendulums and tension traverses, essentially leaning and swinging off the rope to move sideways over blank or unclimbable rock. Soon climbers were constructing ladders of pitons into which they would clip runged rope stirrups, or "etriers", stepping up and slamming home each new piton in turn. This "direct aid" tech-

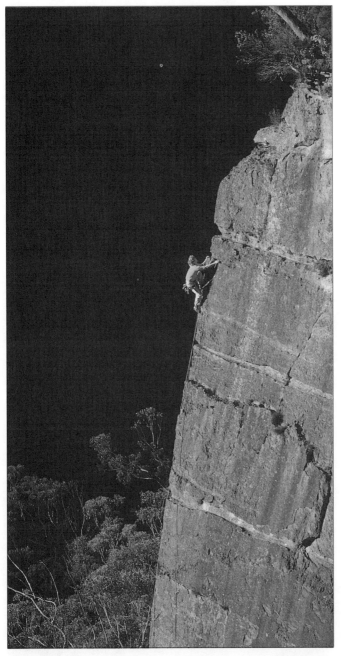

On the edge, Angus MacGuillicuddy lofts up "Who'd rather be sailing?" (5.8), Blue Mountains, Australia. Oftentimes, sensational climbing and bracing locations are found on aretes and sharp, outside corners.

John Sherman photo

nique allowed passage over rock otherwise impossible using only hands and feet. The eventual refinement of this technique led to the first ascents of the finest pure rock walls in the world, in Yosemite Valley, California. And as the standards rose in aid, or "artificial" climbing, so did those in free climbing.

In the U.S. and England, free climbing and aid climbing

were always considered different and distinctive forms. With aid climbing, you used gear as your means of ascent—anything goes. With free climbing, you never used the gear except to safeguard against a fall, and even the slightest infraction—resting on a piton, stepping on a bolt—meant you were not free climbing, but aid climbing. This attitude is based on the concept that artificial and free climbing are distinct pursuits. One is mechanical, the other athletic. No one argued that free climbing was the purer form, and active climbers stuck by the rules, for a game without rules is meaningless. From the beginning (when alpinists shunned assistance from the hemp), climbers were aware that runaway technology, and dependence on it, would dilute the challenge, so the elements of style were upheld to preserve it. Even on routes requiring extensive aid climbing, pioneers would push the free climbing to the limit before breaking out the etriers as a last resort.

The rules of free climbing, unofficial as they were, brought several points to bear. The spirit of adventure and exploration was the very stuff that animated climbing. Furthermore, since one could conceivably hammer their way up any rock wall using aid techniques, free climbing would have to display some element of honesty and fair play —sportsmanship, if you will—lest the two forms become blurred, and the distinctions insignificant. Some big climbs were obviously aid routes, and were approached accordingly. But when there was some doubt, climbers harked back to the original alpinists, when the climber was expected to "climb his own peak", not by hanging on the rope, or pitons, but through his own physical prowess and skill.

On a prospective free route, an honest free climber avoided anything which could reduce the adventure and challenge: he wouldn't descend the climb first, inspecting the rock for available holds, placing protection in the crux sections, chipping footholds, or anything else which could make his ascent easier, or give him unnatural advantage before he had actually taken the lead. He would start from the ground and deal with obstacles as he encountered them—"on sight". If he fell off, he would lower back to the belay and try again, rather than hang on the protection before carrying on. If he was a real stickler, he would pull the rope through the protection and lead it from the ground. If it simply couldn't be free climbed, then aid climb it they did and right on their heels there would be others trying to free it, often succeeding.

Leading climbers stuck fast to the "on sight" philosophy, though as early as 1960, people were pre-inspecting leads on rappel and placing bolts for ready protection once they decided to lead the climb. But these efforts were generally considered as "cheating" and were overlooked by most leading climbers. By 1975, the hardest climbs were so severe that climbers often had to return several times before they could do them legitimately—climbing from belay to belay with no falls and no assistance from the gear. By 1980, the top climbs were still harder, requiring weeks, even months before a "hardman" could make it in one go. To reduce the time spent, climbers started top-roping (belayed from above) the climbs before leading them, pre-placing pro to make the eventual lead less strenuous and dangerous, and rehearsing the moves while hanging on gear (hang-dogging), and in several pitiful instances, manufacturing holds where there were none. Presently, the hardest free routes are sometimes dangerous but, owing to the climbers having memorized every toe hold, every crystal, every thumb position, they are far less adventures than remarkable examples of rock gymnastics. The ultimate goal of any climber is to still climb the route as though the rope was not there—climbing the route without falls (a flash ascent) on the first attempt. However, today's hardest routes are so extreme that most find the old rules impractical, if not passe, but you *do* eventually have to climb the route from bottom to top, no falls, to claim a "free", or "red-point" ascent. The methods used to get there, the how of it all, are immaterial if they serve the end of the "honest" free ascent. So, at least, says the new wave ace. There are a handful of traditionalists who still say any divergence from the old norms is an earmark of a "yellow" climber. Both schools have a point, and the issue remains an ethical quagmire, as it should.

So what does this all mean to the novice? Not much. In fact, it means precious little to anyone save the world-class climber who has his whole existence invested in rock climbing and little else. The novice should approach a climb trying to carry out the old norms, not resting on the protection unless he has to, realizing that top climbers bend the rules because their game is really a different thing altogether. And while the old "on-sight" rules have been somewhat abridged by the cutting edge, even they observe two golden edicts: never place new bolts on existing routes, and never chisel holds into the rock. These "edicts" are the only rules which have sure ethical import, because they can directly, and permanently, effect someone else's experience. A route is public property, and once a route is established, it is no one else's task to change it to their liking. Can you imagine going to the Getty museum and taking hammer and chisel to a Grecian frieze, hammering off the odd mole, straightening an aquiline nose, until you had it just as you liked. You'd be ushered out behind the shed where the big fellas would rearrange *your* features.

As long as you climb with nuts, you are totally free to do as you choose, and nobody is going to care much. Most climbers find that respecting the old rules is more satisfying than making a joke of them. A novice will concern himself with routes that will challenge him, but which he can do without hang-dogging or pre-inspecting. These techniques are reserved for the best on the hardest. If you stick with climbing you will discover all this for yourself and if you find yourself hanging on the protection, no need to tell the priest. Just realize you're not climbing as well as you might be.

Free Soloing

By definition you are free soloing any time you climb without a rope, regardless of the difficulty. The common usage however, refers to a climber who is scaling a fifth class climb where a rope and equipment are usually employed. Yet the free soloer has neither. Only a pair of boots, a chalk bag, and the prowess he brings to the cliffside. Insofar that the penalty for a fall is almost certain death on a route of any length, even experts will question the sanity of the campaign. To the person not given to risk-taking, even the most passionate explanation will ring hollow. Remember, free soloing is rarely a reckless practice, rather a very calculated, conscious act. And it's a matter of degrees. The chances of a 5.12 climber falling off minimal 5.10 terrain are very remote, but still possible. Yet the nervy aficionado will sometimes push the gamble ever closer to his all-out limit till he is virtually doing a high wire act above infinity, where a moment's lapse in concentration, an imprecise toe placement, a fractured rugosity, and the reaper falls. To the novice witnessing this first hand, it seems the purest madness. Why do it? You should certainly not attempt it to find out why. The few who regularly practice free soloing are inevitably experts who technically know exactly what they are doing, and intuitively know exactly why.

What the free soloer craves is either raw intensity, or the joy and freedom that comes from mastery. If he craves notoriety for his feats he is motivated by sham values and may pay for his vanity. The reasons to free solo must come from the heart and be monitored by an icy, analytical mind. Anything else courts disaster. We all climb, amongst other reasons, because it is exciting. So when the free soloer ups the ante to include all the marbles, you can imagine how the thrill is magnified manyfold. Foolish? Perhaps, but an element of tomfoolery runs through the very skein of any climbing. The free soloer has simply pushed things to their ultimate expression. His rewards, in terms of intensity of experience, are the greatest. And so are the penalties. Amazingly enough, very few free soloing accidents ever occur. This is a clear testament that the practice is undertaken by experts in a very measured and sober way. Ultimately free soloing is a distinctively personal affair, and even daily practitioners discourage the practice, as they should. There is certainly no reason for the recreational climber to ever even consider it.

Getting Down

A million postcards feature a colorfully clad climber "roping down" the sheer crag, bounding in arcs, meters off the wall, a waterfall cascading in the background. To the layman, the image embodies everything quixotic about climbing, though there is no climbing involved. Beginning climbers are anxious to try, though this zeal falters as they backpeddle toward the precipitous lip. Climbing manuals are quick to state how experienced climbers hate rapelling. In reality, most climbers don't really mind rapelling, though they avoid it if possible. There is the uncoiling of ropes, setting anchors and sometimes leaving gear behind, the spooky task of absolutely trusting the gear, rarely with any backup. If the rappels are long and involved, including many anchor transfers and a lot of eerie dangling on the gear, even the best climbers will walk a long way to avoid the hassles.

"Abseil" (European), "rappel" (American), "roping down"—call it what you want, it all involves using friction to descend a rope.

Statistically, rappeling is climbing's most dangerous process. A climber's bulk is continuously stressing the equipment, and if any link in the weighted chain should fail, the result is disastrous. Equipment failure, anchors pulling, knots coming untied, and a host of human errors—usually avoidable—have caused many rappeling tragedies. Consequently, assiduous attention must be paid to every aspect of the procedure, starting with choosing the best rappel route.

The Line of Descent

The first question is: Where are you rappeling to? If you're simply heading for the ground and can see that the rope reaches, your task is relatively simple. If you have to make more than a single rappel to reach the ground or your destination, make certain of several things. Are you descending to a ledge, a stance, or what? Do the ropes reach, and if so, what will be the next anchor? Do you have the necessary gear to rig an anchor? Many times rappel routes are established featuring fixed anchors; other times they are not. Many climbs end at a place from which you can walk off. If not, the way down often rappels the route just climbed. You know the topography, the ledges, the anchors. There is no mystery to it.

If you want to descend a virgin stretch of rock, requiring numerous rappels, you have no way of knowing if there are adequate ledges and anchors. Even if you have inspected it with a telescope and can spot a big ledge, you still have no idea how good the anchors might be. Unless you carry a huge bolt kit, you are committing yourself to a real crap-shoot that could leave you stranded. I highly advise you to pass on such an expedition.

For normal sport climbing, you need to know the place you're heading for, that there is an anchor or the possibility of getting one, that the same is available below—all the way to the ground—and that your rope will in turn reach every rappel point. Most guidebooks supply this information, but more often than not your judgement about a situation is what will get you down safely. At many popular crags it is a good idea to ask around if you have any doubts about the way down. When in total doubt always try to rappel the established route, or the route you've just climbed if you have to rappel at all.

ANCHORS

A bomb-proof anchor is the foundation of sane climbing, and the same is true concerning the rappel. Yet several times every year climbers—if not entire teams—are killed because of failed rappel anchors. Occasionally these tragedies are due to acts of God—trees inexplicably coming uprooted, several bolts or pitons popping mysteriously, but more often than not the accidents occurred because someone chose to save equipment and chance it with a suspect anchor. Is the anchor unquestionably sound? It has to be. Go with an indisputable natural anchor whenever possible—a towering ponderosa pine, for instance. With an artificial anchor, a minimum of two nuts, bolts, or pitons are obligatory. Three, even four, different points are sometimes called for, depending on the quality of the placements.

Fixed Anchors

Inspect fixed anchors as if your life depends on them, because it does. Rusty pitons and bolts are particularly suspect. When in doubt, back up the existing anchor or place your own; The cost of a good nut is a small price to pay to assuredly live longer, and all those who follow will benefit by your sacrifice.

At popular climbing areas bolt anchors are sometimes connected by a chain. Never loop your rope around the chain, for if a link or bolt hanger breaks, the rope will slip right off the chain. That happened 1,000 feet up El Capitan, and three young men died. Many times, fixed anchor slings will come equipped with a girthy metal ring, like a medallion, through which you can feed the rope. These rappel rings are nice to pull a rope through and are usually quite strong—the cast aluminum ones are the best—but beware the welded steel ones; a new nylon runner threaded through the eyes or hangers of the anchor isn't given to invisible cracks or work hardening. I've heard of those rings breaking, but I've never heard of a new runner breaking on a rappel.

Most often on fixed rappel anchors, the individual placements—be they nuts (rare), pitons, or bolts—have a host of runners threaded through them from past rappels. The rope is retrieved by pulling it through these slings, and the process can cause enough friction to greatly reduce the strength of the slings. Recently, some old slings taken from rappel anchors were tested for tensile strength, and it's reassuring to know that many of the slings were stronger than expected. Figures indicate that if there are more than four slings in place, there is little chance of all of them breaking. However, wear from the elements, cutting on sharp bolt hangers, and friction burns all factor in to diminish a runner's strength, so the importance of backing up suspect slings cannot be overstated.

Wherever the anchor is, you are obliged to rappel directly below it. Gravity deems it so. A weight on the end of a string hangs directly below the string's anchor. After you have descended a way, you can traverse around a bit, but a slip might set you on a dangerous, sideways tumble. So if you have to rig your own anchor, do so directly above—or as close as possible to—where you plan to descend and don't deviate more than necessary.

Barring special circumstances, you will always rappel on a doubled rope, or ropes, which are retrieved by pulling them through the anchor slings. To facilitate this retrieval, the point where the rope runs through the slings is of vital concern. If you are on a smooth wall, it makes little difference. On a ledge, if the anchor is low, the slings should ideally extend just over the lip of the ledge, so the rope is not bent over a sharp or angled edge. Even the smoothest rappeler will bounce on the rope, which will abrade over an edge, leaving a pile of sheath fiber on the rock. A sharp edge may even cut into the rope. Be keenly aware of what the rope runs over, avoiding, blunting, or even padding any hazards. And make certain the rope is not running through—or even near—any notches, cracks, flakes, or knobs. When it comes time to retrieve the ropes, they will invariably get lodged in these features. And of course inspect the ledge for loose or rotten rock. The action of a rappel can dislodge them, and when you are pulling the ropes down, the free end can whisk loose rocks directly onto you.

Anchor slings should be arranged to hang at less than a 90-degree angle (bottom) to maintain their maximum strength. The weight of the rappeler unduly loads the broadly slung configuration illustrated at top.

On a big ledge you can't extend a runner over the edge since no one carries twenty-foot slings with them. So if the anchor is located some way back from the lip of the ledge, rig the anchor as high as you can above that ledge—say at eye level. This reduces the angle at which the rope passes over the edge, decreasing the friction on the sheath during the descent and on the whole line when you eventually pull it through the anchor. When the rope makes a sharp bend, it tends to bind on the lip, on itself, even in the slings, and retrieval is difficult, sometimes impossible. If this is unavoidable, have the first man down try and pull the ropes from below before the other climbers rappel. Ideally the ropes will have fluid action through the slings, but expect some friction. A nylon rope running over nylon slings will generate friction no matter what the set-up. If the ropes won't budge, try leaving two biners through the slings. If this doesn't reduce the friction enough for retrieval, you'll have to improvise, possibly tying all your slings together so they extend further out. And don't carry on until the ropes can be pulled from below.

Setting the Ropes

If you are making a short rappel, where one doubled rope will do, thread one end through the anchor slings, match it with the other end, and draw the rope through until the middle of the rope is at the slings. Do not drag the rope over the slings. The friction will burn them. Rather, gingerly draw the rope through, an arm's length at a time. Most ropes have a middle mark, but to be certain, it's best to grab both ends, and keeping them together, draw the rope through, knowing you will end up at the middle.

If you are using two ropes, draw one end through the slings and tie it to the end of the second rope using an overhand knot. The knot is strong, easy to tie and untie, and has the happy quality of pulling easily over edges, unlike just about any other knot. When combining ropes of dramatically different diameters, however, a better knot is the double figure-eight follow-through—basically a variation on the already familiar figure-eight. (Another viable knot is the double fisherman's knot—plenty strong, but tough to untie once

(above and below)
Overhand knot

Figure-eight
follow-through

weighted.) Naturally, the knot will be on one side of the anchor. Note this, and remember which rope you must pull to retrieve the ropes. Pulling the wrong rope entails trying to pull the knot through the slings, which is impossible, and often binds or twists the rope in the slings. Then you're stuck and may have to reclimb the pitch to retrieve the rope.

To toss the ropes down, both lines should be neatly piled with ends on top. Normally, you will grab the ends and coil a 40 or 50-foot section of doubled rope and throw this off. This quarter-coil has some heft, and the momentum of the tossed line is usually enough to drag down the remaining line. To get a rope down a broken cliff, where danger of hangup is real, try lap coiling, then tossing the upper half of the rope first, following with the lap-coiled ends.

Carefully inspect the rock below for anything the rope can be snagged on. Gauge your throw to avoid them if possible, even if you must pitch the rope some way to the side. It should straighten out once you start down. If the ropes get bound on some feature—a bush, for instance—and you cannot pull them back up for another toss, you'll have to straighten them out during the rappel. This happens.

You must make certain that the rope reaches the ground or the next anchor. You can normally verify this visually. If not, tie a big knot (double figure-eight) in the end of the rope. Most climbers do this as a matter of course, for rappelling off the end of the rope is not unheard of, and is usually

tossing the rope

If there is doubt the ropes will reach, knot the ends, and for extra assurance , clip an old carabiner through that.

fatal. If the knot is too small, you can rappel right through it. Clipping an old carabiner through the knot is the surest prevention.

RAPPEL BRAKES

There are various devices connecting the rope to the climber that create sufficient friction to allow smooth descent down the rappel line. Properly rigged, rappeling is not strenuous, and the speed of your descent is easily controlled by one hand.

Dulfursitz, or "Body Rappel"

The body rappel is the only method that uses no devices—just the rope—and though rarely called upon, is the only viable means down a rope when other methods or gear is not available. Facing the anchors, straddle the rope. Bring the rope from behind you and across one hip, up across the chest and over the head to the opposite shoulder, over and down the back to the opposite hand, next to where the rope passes over your hip. The rope then makes an "S" and as with all rappels, the up-hill hand is the "guide" hand, the down-hill hand the "brake" hand. The brake hand can easily regulate speed: Moving it out off the back to go faster, pulling it in around the hip to slow down. Most climbers prefer for the brake hand to clasp the rope palm up.

The body rappel is a last resort. Unless you have thick clothing under every inch of passing rope, you'll feel pain—at best. Normally, a beginning climber will make a couple body rappels and never make another all his climbing days—but he will know how. Caught without gear and with a short, relatively low angle way below, the climber with knowledge of the body rappel has a safe means down. But aside from an old timer showing how it's done, or a novice learning how, I've never seen someone intentionally using a body rappel in nearly 20 years of sport climbing. The potential for pain, and the effectiveness of other techniques have made the body rappel obsolete. Besides, by its definition, being without mechanical connection to the rope, you can fall out of the body rappel.

Carabiner Brake

The most popular and efficient method for several reasons, this system uses equipment you already have on your rack. And it is easy to rig. Friction is adjusted by adding or subtracting "braking" carabiners and, properly set up, it's virtually fail safe.

Clip either a large diameter locking biner, or two regular biners—gates opposed—into your swami or harness. To this, clip in two more biners, gates opposed. This second group forms the "platform" for the "braking" biners. To set up the rappel, face the anchor and, straddling the ropes, pull a bight of rope up through the platform biners. Clip the braking biners—gates down—over the platform biners and under the bight of rope.

A single brake biner usually provides enough friction when rappeling on two 11mm ropes. On vertical or overhanging rappels, you'll want two. Rappeling on two 9mm ropes or a single 11mm rope, you may want three brake biners. Your weight, plus how much braking you do with the brake hand, will determine how many braking biners work best for various rappels. Several rappels will tell you what works best for you. Two biners as the brake is the place to start.

Oval carabiners are much easier to use for both the platform and the brake. D's will work, but when the gates are opposed, the contrasting shapes reduce the space for the bight, and are usually a hassle to get clipped. The carabiner brake rappel is very basic and simple, but it can be set up incorrectly. *Never* use only one biner for the platform and be certain to reverse the gates. The bight must pass over the back of the brake biners, not the gates, or the system is lethal.

Rappel Devices

There are legions of belay devices which double as rappel devices. Some years ago the infamous "brake bar", a device lifted from spelunking, was intended to replace the brake biners in a carabiner brake rappel. They were superfluous, sometimes broke, and were thankfully forgotten. Though adequate, belay devices—when used for rappeling—can bind the rope and overheat, and are generally, though not always,

CARABINER BRAKE

1. Two sets of doubled biners, gates opposed.

2. A bight of rope goes through,

3. brake biners are clipped on,

4. clipped over to the other side, and your brake is on.

inferior to the carabiner brake for long rappels.

Aside from the carabiner brake, the "figure eight descender" is the only device I highly recommend for use in any rappeling situation. No less than a dozen companies manufacture them, each with modifications, but the basic design is the same across the board. Lightweight and simple to rig, a figure eight provides the safest and smoothest rappel possible. A novice will note how advanced climbers carry a very minimal rack, nothing extra. But if there's a steep rappel to make, and a figure eight is available, they'll borrow it, though they might not own one themselves.

Figure eight descender

To rig the figure eight, pull the rappel rope through the big hole and loop it around the stem, then clip the small hole into your harness with either a locking biner, or two regular biners, gates opposed. On single ropes, you can feed the rappel rope through the smaller hole, though this often results in excessive friction. If you buy a figure eight, make sure it's good to at least 3,000 pounds, and buy the lightest one you can.

The Rappel Fundamentals

Your hands have separate jobs. The uphill, or "guide" hand is used mainly for balance, and should never death-grip the rope. It can't stop you, and you're only instinctively trying to duplicate the friction that the carabiners or device are creating. The other hand, the "brake" hand, determines your speed. Most climbers keep their brake hand well below their hip, with the rope sliding over it. When they want more speed, they move the rope out and off the hip; to slow down or stop, they wrap the rope back around the hip.

Once you are set up and ready to go, make certain any gear or clothing is well clear of the friction device and cannot get entangled no matter what you do. Long hair must be securely tied back. Anything loose can be drawn into the brake system, and it happens so fast that a whole shirt tail or half a pate can be snatched into the brake with only one downward step. Extraction is very involved, often dangerous, and in the case of hair, always very painful. In most cases, when something has been sucked into the braking device, it becomes locked so tight that the climber is incapable of freeing himself, and a rescue is necessary.

The crux of rappeling is often getting started, particularly if you must descend over a lip. Once the rope is weighted, backpedal to the brink. Keeping your feet there, let out some rope until you are leaning well back. Don't move your feet down too soon. Stability is gained by having your weight pressing straight into the wall, requiring you to maintain a near perpendicular angle relative to the wall. Much less and your feet will skid off and you'll smack the wall. After you have leaned back far enough and feel your weight driving into the wall, slowly pedal back, letting out rope and maintaining your perpendicular angle. The moment you are established on the wall, bend your upper torso in, but keep the legs perpendicular to the cliff. Keep your feet spread apart at shoulder's width for a good foundation. To see where you're going, slightly twist your upper torso towards your brake hand so you can look down.

The aim is a smooth descent, for several reasons. Heroic bounding moves or jerky action stresses the whole system unnecessarily.

Proper rappel posture, angled back, feet spread slightly, and looking down.

Too much speed heats up the friction apparatus and can singe the rope's sheath, making it brittle and stiff to the touch. Inching down is pointless. It wastes everyone's time and usually means you are overgripping with the guide hand. Small steps, fluid action, keeping your eyes below to see your way, and always keeping your legs perpendicular to the cliff; these are the fundamentals of a safe rappel.

A beginner's first few rappels should be accompanied with a belay from above. If there is a problem, the climber is still on belay, which can give a trembling beginner enough confidence to try again. Usually just a couple of belayed rappels is sufficient to get the knack, and you can dispense with the belay.

Overhanging, "Free" Rappels

When the rappeler is hanging in free space with nothing for his feet, the rope should run between the legs, under one leg and up to the brake hand. The added friction of the rope running under the leg in considerable, and providing your

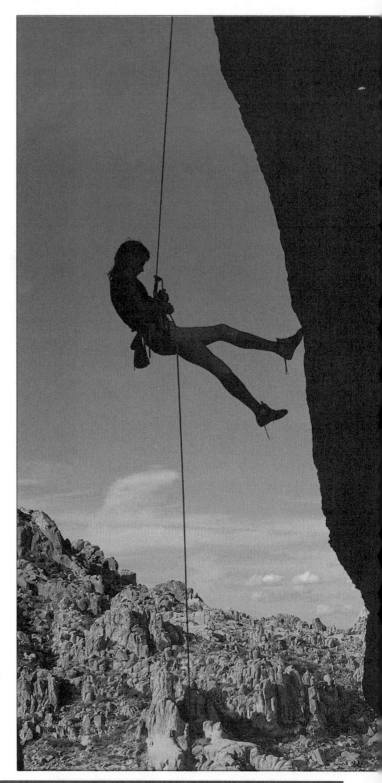

Rappel on! High above an arid rampart, a climber glides into the free rappel on Ryolite Spire, Superstition Mountains, Arizona, With the legs out and the torso bent slightly up, a free rappel is a pleasurable affair, providing the system is prudently rigged.

Bill Hatcher photo

rappel apparatus is giving adequate friction, you can easily stop by folding the rope over the leg. However, try to maintain a smooth, steady descent: If you go too slowly you'll tend to twirl on the rope. Maintain the same posture you would while sitting in a chair. A little tension from your guide hand will keep your upper torso upright.

As you come back in contact with the rock, extend the legs out like antennas, and slowly ease back onto the wall. Never race down a free rappel and suddenly stop. The quick deceleration generates enormous stress on the whole system, and unnecessarily elongates the rope which will abrade over even the smoothest lip.

Safety Back-ups

If for some reason you are doubtful of controlling your rappel and are forced into making one—without a belay—you can rig a back-up with either of two knots that bind on the rope when weighted but can be slid along the rope when not. The traditional knot is the prusik, but this requires rope smaller in diameter (and softer in nature) than the climbing rope, and nut slings are rarely long enough to work. In lieu of cord, $^9/_{16}$-inch sling material will not work effectively as a prusik, but the sling can be combined with a carabiner to form a Bachmann knot that serves the same purpose. Rig the prusik or Bachmann on the rope and attach it with a sling to a locking biner on your waist. When rappeling, cup

Should there be need while rappelling to stop and free the hands, a couple wraps of the rope around a leg will do the trick.

Prusik knot

the guide hand loosely over the knot, sliding it down as you go. Make sure the sling is not too long. If you do go out of control and the knot jams tight, it must be within reach to loosen or you're stuck. And remember that unless the knot jams tight the moment you start sliding it will never jam, but will burn through.

A sliding knot back-up (commonly referred to as a prusik back-up) is rarely if ever used as a normal procedure. If you don't know how to rappel, get a belay. If you are doubtful that you can make a certain rappel don't make that rappel. Only if you are doubtful and must rappel, and no belay is possible, should you consider the prusik back-up as a viable option. Of the few times I've seen the prusik back-up used, the prusik once got jammed so tight that the climber could not loosen it and had to be rescued. But better that than injury.

There is another technique to secure a rappeler of questionable experience, or someone who is injured. Called the "Army Belay", it is quite effective—more so than the prusik back-up because it doesn't have the potential of the jammed or burnt knot. The first person down the rappel applies bodily weight to the end of the rappel rope. The weight creates remarkable added friction on the braking apparatus and can stop the heaviest rappeler cold: He is effectively belayed from below. Mild tension is usually enough. Slack on the rappel rope and the rappeler can carry on normally. Of course, the first rappeler down cannot benefit from this technique, and it does not safeguard a failed or incorrect brake set-up.

Retrieving the Rope

Before the last person comes down he must first double check several things: which rope to pull; is the doubled rope crossed on itself or binding on the slings; is it clear of all notches, grooves, loose rock, and the like. As mentioned, if there is any doubt the ropes can be pulled from below, make certain they can before the last man descends. To facilitate easy retrieval, the last man should separate any twists or kinks in the two ropes so they both run untangled to the ground or next anchor. You can most easily do this by keeping a finger of your guide hand between the two ropes as you descend. On the way down, note any flakes, trees, or blocks that the rope could get entangled with or perhaps pull off upon retrieval.

If you're on the ground, grab the end and walk away from the cliff with it before you start pulling. This gives you a better angle to pull from and decreases wear on the line. It also decreases the chance of dislodging any loose rock. Don't jerk the rope but pull smooth and steadily. As you draw in more line, the rope will often snake down and through the anchor on its own. Whatever the case, once the rope has been freed, always yell "ROPE!" The end of the pulled-through rope can lash like a bull whip and people should be forewarned.

On multiple rappels, feed the free end through the new anchor sling as you pull the rope through the upper anchor. This avoids you having to re-tie the knot at every rappel.

The Bachmann knot, an alternative to the prusik, for use with flat webbing.

Stuck Line

Sometimes the rope gets hung up regardless of the best laid lines. First, be certain that you are pulling the correct rope; it won't work to try and pull the knot through the anchor. Next, flip the rope side to side. If that doesn't clear it, try flipping a loop up the rope straight out, giving one end a stout jerk when the ropes are away from the wall. If all else fails, get everyone to pull on the rope with all their might. That will either free it or, more often, jam it even worse. But since the other options are pretty grievous, try it anyway.

If the rope is honest-to-God stuck fast, you have several options. If you still have both ends of the rope, tie both ends off to the new anchor and prusik up one or the other lines. If you have retrieved all or enough of one rope and the very end of the second line is mysteriously hung up (this does happen), you can re-lead the pitch on the free rope. If you only have one end and not much slack, your task is pretty hateful, but possible. You must tie off your end to the new anchor, fit a sturdy prusik on the rope, and re-lead the pitch by moving the prusik up the rope and placing protection below it. If you fall, the rope is tied off, the prusik will hold, and you are held by any protection you have placed below the prusik. It is also a good idea to tie into the rope from time to time with a figure eight or butterfly knot to back up the prusik. If you are ever forced into this position, don't worry about style. Liberally cheat, hang on every nut and place plenty of them. Do whatever is necessary to safely gain the snag.

If all else fails, yell for help. If somebody is easily available, certainly get their assistance before trying the prusik-lead. If the ropes are stuck on top of a cliff or outcrop, there are often climbers milling about, and a jammed line can be freed in seconds. A climbing team must be self-reliant, but everybody gets a rope stuck sometime and there's no shame in getting a hand if it's easily gotten and the options are dangerous.

Getting Back Up

If you rappel to a stance that has no place to anchor, you will have to ascend the rappel rope if you cannot climb back up. Rig two prusiks or Bachmann knots—one tied *within arm's reach* to your harness, the other to a sling into which both feet may be cinched. Procedure: Pull up legs, slide up lower knot, stand up while sliding top knot up. Repeat. Though relatively simple, you will want to practice this before you need to use it. It would likely be in an emergency, a very poor situation in which to be learning new techniques. Because of the somewhat capricious nature of prusiks, it is important to tie into the rope periodically during your ascent with a figure eight or butterfly knot. Be certain of your anchor before you simply prusik up the rope; if it is simply a snagged line, prusik-lead the pitch as described above.

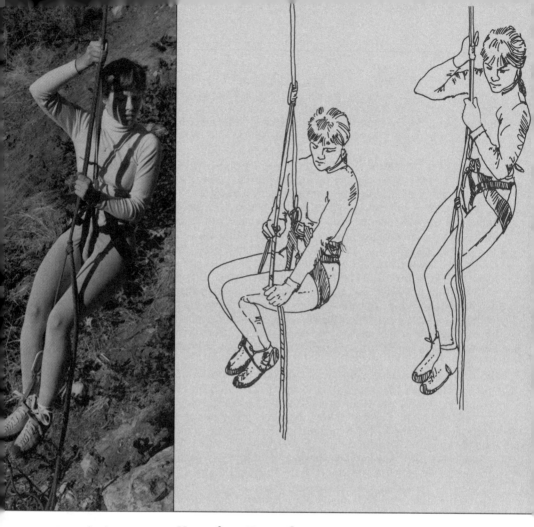

Hanging Transfers

Getting back up a rope with two prusiks or Bachmann knots is fairly simple and comfortable with a harness or leg loops. Be sure to tie into the rope from time to time, however, because prusiks can slip, and when they do, they can fail. Tie an overhand knot into a bight of rope and clip this into your harness.

Now that you understand the basic procedure, we can look at the most demanding of all rappel situations: rappeling down a steep wall with no ledges or even stances. This procedure is most common for climbers who are retreating from big climbs, but is also encountered by anyone who is rappeling a route with a hanging belay. The procedure is complicated and the potential for error is high, so it is essential that every precaution is taken.

Assume that the anchor is fixed, say three bolts. Because there is no ledge, you must tie a knot into the end of the rappel ropes to insure you don't rappel off the end. Once you gain the anchor, you must tie yourself in, independently of the ropes. There are several methods to do this. The most secure is to clip biners into all three bolts and secure yourself to them with a sling threaded through your swami or harness. Only after you have done so should you unclip from the rappel rope, immediately securing the rappel rope to the anchor. As the second climber rappels down, you must rig a sling through the three bolts that will serve as the anchor for the next rappel. When the second climber arrives at the anchor, he must secure himself to the anchor independently of the rope, also with a sling running from his harness or swami. Once you have pulled the rope through the upper anchor and fed it through the new sling at your present anchor, the first rappeler rigs his rappel before he unclips from the anchor. When the last man rappels, he must remove the biners from the bolt hangers. He might find it useful to clip a sling into the rappel sling, and stand in it to get enough height to remove the biners. Then he rappels down.

Conclusion

Because rappeling is so easy to do, climbers sometimes race through the set-up, and the annual accident report is grim evidence of their haste. Like a jet pilot, the wise climber goes through a pre-rappel check list that runs like this: Is his harness secure, knots and buckles tight? Is the anchor bombproof? Are the slings strong enough and tied correctly—particularly if you're using someone else's rappel slings? Are the ropes tied together properly? Do they reach the ground or next anchor? Is the braking system rigged correctly? Are loose clothes, gear, or hair far out of the way? Is the line of descent free of loose or rotten rock? Will the lines pull through okay? With a little experience, it only takes moments to check and double check these things. Don't become a mother's lament; get in the habit of checking and double-checking every phase.

COILING THE ROPE

Anyone who has spent time on a sailboat knows that the scoundrel who haphazardly coils a rigging line, if found out, spends the rest of his tour bailing bilge water, polishing the

Free hand coil (left), and coiling over the knee.

toilet lid, or is simply pitched overboard. The climber who haphazardly coils the rope is twice a chump, for it's an easy task and only takes a few minutes to do properly. A poorly coiled rope is a polecat to untangle and can take several people half an hour of steady cursing to get straight.

There are several different methods of coiling a rope. Most common is the standing coil. Leaving a tail of a couple feet, form successive coils about five feet, or two arm's breadth long. The fastest, and worst, method is to coil the rope with two free arms. Next best is to sit and coil it around a foot and knee. The best method is to coil it around your neck. As you coil, shake out any kinks and twists. With a very kinky rope, another climber should help shake out the line, leaving you to coil it. If the rope is incomprehensibly twisted, you might have to walk it out and twirl it about to get it straightened. Normally this happens only to old ropes that have just been rappeled on, where the sheath had shifted around. Best to get a new rope, though a new rope will also kink until it's broken in. Another common way to coil the rope is the "mountaineer's coil". This is best when you don't have a pack and you need maximum arm freedom—to do some scrambling, say.

DOWNCLIMBING

In the previous chapter we encouraged skills in down-climbing on the lead. Competent downclimbing is also essential to descend gullies, slabs, chimneys, or any stretch of rock encountered once the climb is over, should rappeling not be a safe or practical alternative. You will find that unless the rappel route is very straightforward and hassle free, most experienced climbers will opt to climb down off a crag if a realistic route is available. And even when the rappel route is a simple task, climbers will still climb off. It's often faster, and their fate is in their own hands, not dependent on equipment. Downclimbing can be as fun and challenging as climbing up. Almost without exception, downclimbing is done without a rope since the terrain is usually fairly easy.

The downclimbing route must be free of loose or rotten rock. If it isn't, no one should be in a position to be hit by rockfall. It is generally best to keep the party close together so falling stones do not build momentum, and the first one down can forewarn those behind of particular danger spots. Most climbers will face out, leaning back to the wall with one or both arms if they need balance. When the angle steepens, it's easier to face in, peering past your hip or between your legs for directions. A little experience and all the nuances will come clear.

The ability to downclimb safe and fast is a handy skill. You can outrun approaching storms, avoid unnecessary rappels and, providing you use common sense, have a fun time doing so.

If you start down the wrong gully or shoulder, though, it

STANDING COIL
(opposite page: top)

After coiling the rope, secure the ends with a whip finish; lay the short end back as a loop atop the coil, wind about five or six feet of the other end around, working towards the loop and making sure that each wrap is as snug as you can make it, and finally, finish by pulling the end through the initial loop.

MOUNTAINEER'S COIL
(opposite page, bottom)

To do the mountaineer's coil start by matching both ends of the rope, then lap the doubled rope, leaving the first fifteen feet of the ends uncoiled. With this, wrap around the coil, draw the doubled end through itself as shown, and lay the separate ends over the shoulders and secure the coil by wrapping the remaining ends around the waist.

can get nasty. Against my better instincts I thrashed down a manzanita chocked gully east of Mt. Watkins in Yosemite Valley, and Lord Jim with a chain saw couldn't have reversed it. Five hours and a thousand weeping punctures later we finally gained the valley floor, and I've been careful what I head down ever since.

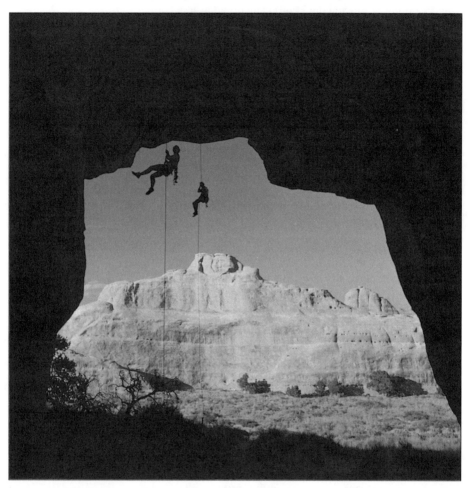

Brother Gaines and John Long simal-rappeling after climbing Pine Tree Arch, Arches, New Mexico. Finding no anchor on top, the stranded climbers simply rappeled off each other, the rope stretched between them and over the wide arch—an emergency drill to be sure.

Gaines collection photo

CHAPTER 7

Training for Climbing

The practice of training for a sport by doing exercises outside the sport itself is nothing new. Called cross-over training, we see it in all professional athletics: skiers run stairs and lift weights; football players run, lift weights, and do stretching exercises to reduce the chance of injury; divers jump on a trampoline and lift weights; swimmers lift weights, jump rope, and ride a stationary bike, as do basketball players. All of these athletes count on their routines to give them a sharp conditioning edge that will "cross-over" to their actual sport.

Few climbers, even those who take it seriously, are motivated enough to train regularly with climbing in mind. The great majority of climbers are only in it for fun, recreation outside the arena, and have lives or work schedules which preclude the necessary time for specialized work-outs. But as the top climbs become increasingly more physical and leading climbers recognize themselves as world-class athletes, the attitudes trickle down into the mainstream. Over the last decade, even week-end warriors have begun hitting the weight room and pull-up bar, hoping to increase their performance. This trend has resulted in the development and supply of training equipment specifically for climbing.

The early apparati had some major drawbacks. The rope ladder, popular about five years ago, resulted in grievous elbow injuries from the wrenching and stress of repeated one arm lowering. Fingertip pull-ups caused joint problems in many. Other devices, like various hand squeezers and finger-tension gadgets, were fine for recovering from injuries, but did little to increase strength or endurance. Many common work outs were geared to gain the strength to do circus feats—like one arm pull-ups—which had surprisingly little positive effect on people's climbing. As certain exercises are being eliminated if they cause injuries and new devices are introduced almost daily, it's still not clear how to attain optimum results while staying injury free. Likewise, it is virtually impossible to discuss various exercises and devices without taking up training philosophies. Still, there are several physiological facts that cannot be denied.

First, strong fingers are every climber's dream. And since the fingers don't have muscles, it's the sinew connections in the forearms (and the attending muscles) that must be strengthened.

Second, most every climbing exercise involves some form of pull-up—duplicating the movement on the rock—and it's the latissimus dorsi, or "lats", which are the prime mover in this action. You simply cannot strengthen the lats alone, though. You must also train the antagonistic muscles required for the pulling movement—the chest and trapezius, even the abdominals—to provide balanced muscled groups and avoid injury. Lastly, any muscle group which you train to failure requires at least 48 hours to recover. These comments are not opinions, but incontrovertible facts that must be factored into any workout. They tell us certain things that have long been overlooked by the climbing world. It is fine to concentrate on the lats and forearms, but not at the exclusion of the other muscles. To do so is to invite injury. And totally blasting those muscles every third day will bring much better results than doing so every day, or every other day.

From this we can conclude that while it is probably desirable to do specialized exercises which closely ape the climbing movement—and focus on the muscle groups most involved—it is likewise important to round out the routine and physique with an equal amount of general conditioning exercises. Anything else results in an unbalanced machine, where weak antagonistic muscles are throwing the whole body out of kilter. For general conditioning, weight training is second to none.

Weight Training

For years climbers scorned weight training, usually for the wrong reasons. Strength-to-weight ratio has long been deemed the aim of all climbing workouts, and most climbers are loath to add any size to their whippet-thin physiques—not knowing that a mere five pounds of brawn might increase their strength upwards of ten per cent. (Also, many people think you can throw on five or ten pounds of muscle with a couple workouts. A dedicated lifter is lucky to add one pound of muscle every two to three months.) Correct weight training is tough duty, certainly more toil than joy, which makes it all the more unpopular. Other misconceptions have also kept many climbers off the iron. The first is the notion of excess bulk. As absurd as it is, people think that weights automatically make you huge. It's food, rather than iron, than increases body size. Controlling one's diet controls size, and you can't eat a dumbbell. Second is the notion of the muscle-bound oaf, who can't comb his hair for all the huge deltoids. If anything, correct weight training—which entails full range exercises and a lot of stretching between sets—increases flexibility. But you have to do things right.

This is not the venue to spell out specific work-out routines. A comprehensive iron routine can be easily designed to focus on a climber's needs. There are hundreds of books and videos to show you what's what. The best routines take account of a person's physique and mentality and are so personal that little applies across the board. For the climber new to weights, it's best to start a normal, conservative routine and customize it as your knowledge increases. Perhaps the best thing with weight training is that it is very difficult to incur serious injuries. Soreness and tweaked muscles are part of any training, but in over fifteen years of being an "iron-rat", I've never once gotten an injury lifting weights that has kept me out of the gym for more than a week.

Free Hand Exercises

Essentially calisthenics, free hand exercises involve all the Jack LaLanne-type routines (save towing the boats): Push ups, pull ups, sit ups, dips. Pretty hard to get a well rounded work out doing just free hand exercises, but they require little in the way of specialized gear and are certainly better than doing nothing. Also, it is hard to injure yourself doing them.

Aerobics, Jazz dancing, swimming, Nautilus machines, and untold other routines are also possible and popular. Anything that promotes overall fitness can only help your climbing.

Cardiovascular Excercises

A strong heart and good wind are vital for strenuous climbs. Any action sport, like basketball or racketball, is good. Pure running or bicycling are also good. But the king of them all is the jump rope, which has steadily gained popularity in the climbing world, probably because it requires a lot of skill to be good. Single revolutions on a rope marks beginning level. Double revolutions, intermediate. Triple revolutions, advanced. The person who can consistently do triple revolutions on a skip rope has the heart of a lion and lungs enough to fill the sails of a good-sized bark. Make sure to get a leather rope.

Specialized Apparati

Hang boards, first introduced in late 1986, are wooden or molded-resin boards (usually about a foot high by $2\frac{1}{2}$ feet long) that are mounted up high like a pull-up bar. The "board" features various holds resembling those on a climb, from good jugs to rounded nothings, and the usual routine

Typical finger board, this one by Entre Prises.

involves pulling up on the holds, as well as free hanging for timed intervals. There are half a dozen commercially available, and each comes with a suggested work out. There is no doubt that they can increase finger, hand, and forearm strength, and that the carry-over value to climbing is high; but the verdict is not yet in on whether they cause more injuries than good. It is probably a matter of the routine. Increasing stress beyond normal climbing levels, especially free-hanging for long periods on the board's punier holds, virtually assures injuries. The primary danger is that the tendon connections at the shoulder—should you be hanging fully extended—have less strength than you can develop with your fingers. This means that as you hang to exhaustion on your fingertips, your body weight naturally sags to the tendon connectors at your shoulder; it is these connectors that risk separating. Adding weights will reduce the time spent on your fingers, and that will tend to keep you off your shoulders, or use elastics or some device to help prevent the transfer of load from muscle to unprotected joint connectors. Whatever routines you decide on, remember that if you push yourself to muscle failure, you need 48 hours to fully recover. So to optimize your results on any board, heavy work outs every third day are far superior to those every day, or every other day.

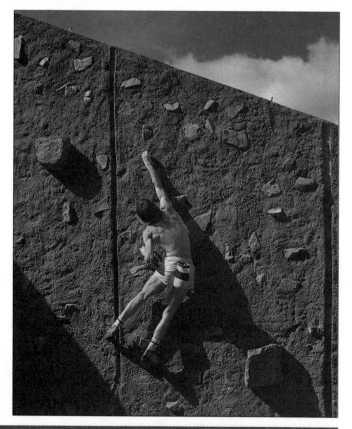

Jeff Smoot pumps up one of the oldest artificial climbing walls in the United States, the University of Washington Practice Rock.

Smoot collection photo

Climbing Walls

Artificial climbing walls—many of them indoors—have been springing up all over the country. Not only do they provide good exercise, they're good fun. Most are big enough that an enterprising climber can traverse up, around, and across one indefinitely, thus simulating the feel and exertion of a long lead. This is not cross training, but climbing itself. Cast out of resin and sand, the holds simulate actual rock very well. In addition, the wide availability of modular holds encourages the indoor creation of home walls in basements and garages. A caution, however: Since many indoor walls try to squeeze "bang for buck" by utilizing only small holds, the routes can be difficult, and it is essential injury prevention to warm up sufficiently before launching off onto the wall. But climbing walls are great places to hone footwork and general technique. And a little friendly competition can push a climber to exhaustion.

Bouldering

Bouldering is essentially climbing on rocks small enough that a rope is unnecessary. The world's hardest climbing—in terms of individual moves and small sequences—has always been, and always will be, done on boulders. The controlled medium, the ease of trying, trying, and trying again, and the ferocious, though mostly friendly competition that surrounds the pastime make ideal conditions for the best climbers to try the hardest sequences imaginable. The first time I saw a world-class boulderer in action I was thunderstruck. I'd been climbing about three months, clawing up easy climbs made all the harder because—in the spirit of the great mountaineers—we bore weighty packs and climbed in hiking boots. And before me was a man in shorts, varappe boots, and a chalk bag, powering up overhanging rock like it was nothing, ever controlled, graceful, with precision and explosive strength that seemed mind boggling. The experience reoriented me in seconds. No more packs, off with the hiking boots—it was time to start sport climbing.

Bouldering is such an engaging and stimulating endeavor that many climbers prefer it to roped climbing. Unquestionably, bouldering is the quickest way to gain climbing skill. A dedicated boulderer brings a lot of artillery to a roped climb. Strong fingers and good footwork, requisite for any difficult bouldering, are his in abundance. But it's the experience of having done thousands of different sequences that gives him the real edge. It's doubtful that an experienced boulderer will encounter anything on a roped climb that he hasn't already done—in some fashion or another—on the boulders. Beginning climbers can master the fundamentals in several months, intermediate climbers can become experts in a year, and experts can maintain their edge with a couple of good bouldering sessions a week.

All bouldering is not low level work, however. High boul-

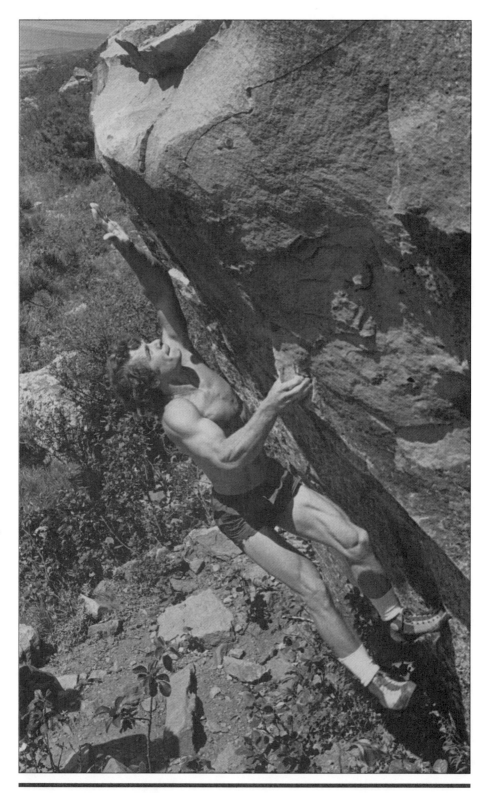

dering, essentially free soloing, has long been a popular game of Russian Roulette amongst experts. For the novice and intermediate climber, you will not want to climb any higher than a point where you feel comfortable jumping off. If you must assume an upside down or awkward position, have a friend spot you. And remember, if you fall off, you hit the ground. Always clear the landing zone of the problem stones or other detritus that could cause twisted or broken ankles—the most common injuries in bouldering. If there is any doubt about the seriousness of a bouldering "problem"—that it's too high—rig a top rope.

Top Roping

Top roping involves rigging an anchor above the desired climb. The rope runs up through the anchor, and back down to the ground—one end for the climber, the other for the belayer. This way a climber can ascend with a belay from above, and a fall is no longer than the stretch in the rope—usually just inches. There are several considerations to bear in mind. The anchor must be bomber and directly above the climb. The anchor sling must extend from the anchor to just over the lip of the climb, allowing the rope to run freely through it. Even if you clip the rope off with locking carabiners, use at least two. Many times it is difficult to find an anchor at the base of boulders. If the angle of the rock is less than vertical, it is often unnecessary for the belayer to use one, though it is always desirable. Stretch in the rope, friction on the top anchor, and his own bulk is often adequate if a ground anchor is unavailable. But if the angle is steep, or there is a discrepancy in weights between belayer and climber, an anchor is useful, particularly for lowering climbers to the ground.

Injuries

As the technical envelope is pushed further, debilitating injuries are becoming more commonplace. Aside from the normal muscle tweaks and strains inherent in any physical endeavor, climbers are particularly prone to elbow and finger injuries, most of which involve some form of tendonitis. Having suffered these impairments on numerous occasions, I can assure you that ignoring the injury can result in pain so intense that straightening the arm, or closing the fingers, is virtually impossible, and climbing is out of the question. Concerning treatment for these conditions, I defer to climber/orthopedist Dr. Mark Robinson, who has conducted several studies involving climbing injuries, and is in the best position to give advice. Writes Dr. Robinson:

"Self cure for tendonitis. 1) Decrease activity until pain is gone, and all swelling and tenderness disappear. 2) Wait two weeks more. 3) Start with easy strength exercises—putty, gum, rubber squeezers (2-3 weeks). 4) Low angle big-hold climbing (1 month). 5) High angle big-hold climbing (1

(page opposite)

John Long cranks the "Pinch Overhang", a classic problem at one of the premier bouldering areas in the world, Horsetooth Reservoir, near Fort Collins, Colorado.

Michael Kennedy photo

month). 6) Back to full bore.

"Anti-inflammatory medicines (aspirin, motrin, nuprin, etc.) can be used to control symptoms and speed the recovery process. They should not be used to suppress pain to allow even more overuse, since this will eventually lead to worse problems and a longer recovery period.

"Various mystical and pseudo-scientific remedies, such as copper bracelets, dietary modifications, herbal cataplasms, spinal manipulations, electrical machines with imposing control panels, horse liniments, ethnic balms, etc., are at best unproven. Very few, if any, of them bear any conceivable relation to what is known to be the basis of the problem."

What the doctor is telling us is that time and patience are the key ingredients to a full recovery, and that returning prematurely to high-stress climbing is as foolish as ignoring an injury in the first place. "The tissues of the musculo-skeletal system are capable of remarkable feats of repair and restoration", Dr. Robinson assures us, "but these processes are slow." Furthermore, there is nothing in known medicine that can accelerate these processes, save the use of anti-inflammatory drugs, which simply eliminate the restrictions and allow the healing to proceed. All the fancy gadgets and therapy are virtually useless for tendon injuries, though any sports medicine clinic will gladly take all the spare coinage one has.

The tendency is to race back onto the cliffside and crank our brains off the second the pain is gone, but experts assure us this can only exacerbate the injury. Do as you want, but I'm taking Dr. Robinson's advice.

Injury Prevention

We know the medical experts have told us that certain exercises virtually assure injuries, and we should avoid these if we're in for the long haul. But aside from that, what can we do? Some support of critical tendons can be achieved by taping. Trouble spots: around the fingers on either side of the main (second) joint, around the wrist, and around the forearm just shy of the elbow. But professional athletes are more and more relying on two things to avoid injuries: stretching and warming up. Aerobics and yoga might not make you stronger, but they may keep you from getting injured. And a very important practice is to do a little stretching, and some easy climbing before jumping onto a hard climb. Warming up is part of any sport, and should be essential for climbers whose movements so stress the elbows and fingers. This is

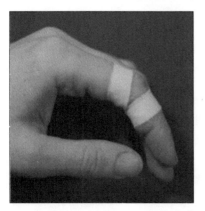

Supporting the finger tendons with tape.

particularly true for bouldering. Get limbered up with a running sweat, then max yourself. And if you tweak something, stop before you make it worse.

Getting
Started
and Staying
Alive

As little as a dozen years ago, finding professional instruction was a difficult task. Today, there is nearly always a guide service/climbing school operating around every popular crag and good instruction is easy to find. For the complete neophyte, I highly advise taking at least a beginning seminar. It allows one to get a good grip on the fundamentals, and is the single most valuable investment a beginner can make. The appendix following this chapter lists sources of information on both instruction and equipment.

For an outlay of about 200 dollars, a beginner can buy a pair of rock boots and two days of professional instruction. If you choose to carry on, you will need to purchase some climbing gear. Richard Leversee of Chouinard Equipment has plotted the following course for the beginner looking to make climbing his sport:

After mastering basic techniques for safety and movement on rock, the novice should seek the company of more experienced partners to advance his skill. After buying a pair of rock shoes, his investment can be minimal, since the new climber can limit his purchases to personal rather than community necessities. The gear listed below will allow the beginner to climb with anyone with a rope and rack (and, of course, the knowledge to use them).

Sit harness or swami w/ leg loops	$45.00
Locking carabiner	$12.00
Belay/rappel device	$15.00
Four oval carabiners @ $6.00 each	$24.00
Gear sling	$8.00
Chalkbag, chalk	$14.00
Total	$118.00

Climbing with others is a crucial learning time, as a novice needs mileage before jumping out on the lead. The opportunity for adventure really opens up once a climber buys a rope and rack. There are many options available in selecting a rope, but the beginner can't go wrong buying either a 10.5mm or 11mm UIAA-approved kernmantle rope from any of the manufacturers listed in the appendix.

A "foundation rack" should include a variety of passive

(non-mechanical) nuts—tapers and hexentrics and the like—for their light weight, simplicity, security, and low price. At this stage it is important to become adept at placing passive nuts. Even spring-loaded camming devices require this knowledge for sound placements. The following foundation rack will allow the climber to set up top ropes and lead most popular easy climbs.

Rope	$130.00
Oval and D carabiners (20 @ $6 each)	$120.00
Set of nuts ($1/4$" to 4" w/ slings)	$130.00
Shoulder length runners (6 @ $2 each)	$12.00
Quickdraw runners (4 @ $2 each)	$8.00
Nut extraction tool	$7.00
Local guidebook	$15.00
Total	$422.00

As the climber builds a solid base of experience, he will naturally want to upgrade the foundation rack, allowing for more versatility and safety. SLCD's, three-cam units, sliding nuts, micro-nuts, and other sophisticated forms of protection will open the door to more difficult climbs.

Micro nuts (2-5, $7.50 each)	$30.00
Three-cam units (five from $5/16$" to $1 1/2$" @ $33.00 each)	$165.00
Spring loaded camming devices ($1 1/8$" to 4", one each)	$220.00
D-shaped carabiners (10 @ $6.00 each)	$60.00
Shoulder-length runners (three @ $2.00 each)	$6.00
Quickdraw-length (short) runners (two @ $2.00 each)	$4.00
Total	$485.00

All told, an advanced leader can have a world-class rack for just over $1,100.00, which makes sport climbing the cheapest of all adventure sports. Moreover, after the initial investment, there are no additional expenses save gas to get to the cliff and minimal fees to climb inside state or national parks. Rock climbing is essentially free: no lift tickets, no referees, nothing but you, your friends, and the challenge at hand.

RESPONSIBILITIES

Throughout rock climbing's evolution, the simple joy of being the master of one's fate, of seeing success or failure as a result of one's efforts has—as in any great sport — remained the heart of the experience. Self reliance and the ability to take responsibility for one's actions are among the virtues that climbing encourages.

But, there are many more climbers out on the cliffs than ever before. The community of climbers—once a small, counter-culture, "outcast" society—now impacts the outdoors in profoundly visible ways. Trails and trash are found at the base of "wilderness" cliffs. The responsibility for this lies with all of us, of course. Part of the allure of rock climbing is that it is more than just a physical exercise; we are intrinsically bound to features that nature has provided us. The environment is fragile, and the responsibility to maintain it is an intedral part of our outdoor experience. The following suggestions address some of these issues.

Serve yourself and others by picking up trash when you find it, whether or not you brought it to the cliffs yourself. Relieve yourself away from the bottom of the route. Make a practice of carrying a small plastic bag into which to carry out all toilet paper and, mindful that uncovered feces decompose faster, keep such deposits well clear of established trails and paths. On longer routes, try to urinate away from where others must climb.

Stick to established trails whenever possible. We know ourselves competent at travelling over the roughest country in pursuit of the most direct line to our selected route; we should more often demonstrate our sensitivity to the effects of rampant erosion that are the result of zealous proliferation of access trails. Nesting birds should be respected and left as we find them. We are guests of the crags and its inhabitants.

Codes of proper cliffside etiquette are, of course, no different than those most people practice in the greater world. There are, however, situations that are unique. Usually, the first party to the base of a route gets the route first. You might offer the route to a clearly faster party, but once on a route, feel under no obligation to let a party pass if for any reason you are not comfortable with them above you. Again, if they are obviously a quicker team, it is probably a nice thing to offer, but if, say, loose rock is an issue, don't feel compelled to let anybody by: they made their choice at the beginning of the route.

As climbing moves into the 1990s and beyond, one of the biggest problems confronting all climbers is access to the cliffs. The loss of access to climbing or bouldering areas is an issue that affects every climber, regardless of technical ability or stylistic preference. The responsibility for solving or preventing access problems likewise rests with each and every climber. Minimizing environmental impact and being sensitive to behavior which could affect access will help prevent problems. When access problems do arise, the Access Committee of the American Alpine Club can help negotiate, organize, and even litigate closures of climbing areas. But, negotiations and litigation can't solve every access problem. For this reason, the AAC Access Fund was established to finance the actual purchase or preservation of climbing and bouldering areas. Your tax deductable contribution to the Access Fund is a concrete way of giving something back to climbing and making a real difference in the effort to save the rich diversity of climbing resources in the United States. To send your donation (of any amount) to the Access Fund, or to contact the Access Committee, write to the American Alpine Club, Post Office Box 67A25, Los Angeles, CA 90067.

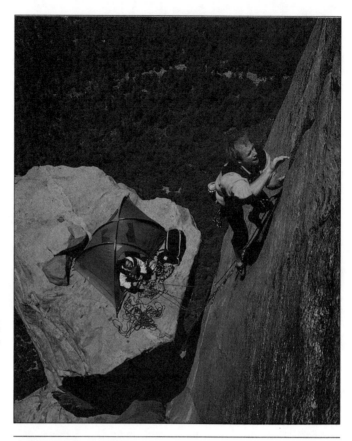

Todd Skinner frees the 21st pitch (5.11c) of El Capitan's Salathe Wall while partner Paul Piana belays atop El Cap Spire.

Bill Hatcher photo

STAYING ALIVE

Rock climbing is potentially hazardous, and it is the responsibility of the individual to learn and understand the proper techniques to insure the safest possible participation.

Though no substitute for professional instruction or experience that only years of climbing can provide, this manual has hopefully helped both the novice and the expert to a greater knowledge of rock climbing's fundamentals and nuances. In summary, I offer part of a longer essay on safety which appeared under the same name in the introduction of the 1987 Yosemite guidebook. Prepared by head rescue ranger, John Dill, the essay contains wisdom distilled from nearly three decades of seeing every kind of accident in every kind of situation by every kind of climber— from rank beginner to world-class hero. To one and all, says John:

State of mind is the key to safety. It's impossible to know how many climbers were killed by haste or overconfidence. Many accident survivors will tell you that, somehow, they lost their better judgement just long enough to get hurt. It's a murky subject. Nevertheless, these mental lapses generally fall under three categories: ignorance, casualness, and distraction.

Ignorance

Even the most conscientious climber can get into trouble if he's unaware of the danger ("I thought it never rained..."). There is always something more to learn, regardless of experience. There are two basic steps to fighting ignorance.

• Continue to read, and listen to climbers who have survived. Back issues of climbing magazines are full of pertinent articles. Case histories in the American Alpine Club's *Accidents in North American Mountaineering,* a yearly compilation of accident reports, will show you how subtle factors may conspire to catch you unaware. Such accounts are the next best thing to being there.

• Practice. Reading may make you aware but not competent. Regardless of the written word, which *is* sometimes wrong, you must ultimately think and act for yourself. Several climbers have waited to learn how to prussik until it was dark, raining, overhanging, and they were actually in trouble. They had read about it, but they still had to be rescued despite having the gear to improvise their own escape. Book-learning alone gave them a complacency that could have proved fatal.

Casualness

"I just didn't take it seriously." It's a common lament. It's often correct, though it's more a symptom than a disease—there may be deeper reasons for underestimating your risk. Ignorance is one. Here are some more.

• Habit reinforcement occurs when nothing goes wrong. The more often you get away with risky business the more entrenched your lazier habits become. Have you unconsciously dropped items from your safety checklist since you were a beginner?

• Your attitudes and habits can be reinforced by the experiences (and states of mind) of others. The sense of awe and commitment of the 1960s is gone from the big-wall "trade routes", and young aspirants with no Grade VI's (or even V's) to their credit speak casually about them. Yet most of the accidents on El Capitan occur on "easy" pitches.

MEMORY DECAY "I'm not going up again without raingear—I thought I would die!" A week later this climber has forgotten how scared he had been in that thunderstorm. Raingear was now too heavy and besides, he'd rap off the next time. Many of us tend to forget the bad points. We have to be hit again.

CIVILIZATION With fixed anchors marking the way and ghetto blasters echoing behind, it may be hard to realize how high the potential danger actually is. Some say the idea of a fast rescue added to their casualness. Maybe, but who wants a broken leg, or worse, in the first place?

OVERCONFIDENCE "It'll never happen to me. I'm a safe, cautious climber". Many of those killed were described by friends as very cautious.

Distraction

It is caused by whatever takes your mind off your work: Fear, thirst, sore feet, skinny-dippers below—the list is endless. Being in a hurry is one of the most common causes. Here are two ways it has happened.

• Experienced climbers have often been hurt after making "beginner errors" (their words) to get somewhere quickly. There was no emergency or panic, but their minds were elsewhere—on a cold beer, a good bivouac, or just sick of being on that route for a week (often called "summit fever"). Their mistakes were usually short cuts in protecting easy pitches, on both walls and day climbs. As one put it, "We were climbing as though we were on top."

• Darkness has caught two day-climbers for the first time. Unprepared, upset, and off route, they rushed to get down, arguing with each other about what to do. After several errors, which they knew to avoid, one climber was killed rappeling off the end of his rope.

• Learn to recognize when you or your partner are becoming distracted. Stop, get your act together, then proceed.

Rescues

Despite the macabre sound of all ranger Dill's observations, the percentage of accident victims is minuscule compared to the hundreds of thousands of active rock climbers. But the dangers are real, and should you or a ropemate be so unfortunate as to suffer injury, Dill has put forth the following concerning rescues:

Despite the best of preparations, an accident can happen to anyone. Self-rescue is often the fastest and safest way out, but whether it's the wise course of action depends on the injury and how well prepared you are. Combining with a nearby party may often give you the margin of safety you need, but do not risk aggravating an injury or getting yourselves into a more serious predicament—ask for help if you need it. Sometimes a bit of advice, delivered through loudspeaker, is all that's required.

If you don't have formal first aid training (which is highly recommended), at least know how to keep an unconscious patient's airway open, how to protect a possible broken neck or back, and how to recognize and deal with a flail chest, external bleeding, and serious blood loss (shock). These procedures are life-saving, do not require fancy gear, and are easy to learn and perform.

• Head injury victims are apt to be irrational and very strong. Even if he's unconscious, if you have to leave him, make it impossible for him to untie himself.

Dave Wright swipes at the mottled ice on "Rigid Designator", near Vail, Colorado. Like many of the more technical ice climbs, the route follows little more than a girthy icicle which comes into shape but a few weeks a year, if that. Note the protection—two ice screws—closely spaced beneath him.

Glenn Randall photo

THE OTHER SIDES OF THE GAME

Climbing is a broad game to which sport climbing is only a part—a fundamental, popular part, but by no means even half the game. Big walls will always provide the most awesome form of pure rock climbing, for the medium—towering monoliths like El Capitan and Mt. Watkins in Yosemite Valley—is peerless for grandeur and intimidation. Huge sixth class routes are steep, often unnerving trials that terrify and amaze twenty-year veterans. They are sometimes three-quarters of a mile high, and a hammock bivouac at that altitude is an ordeal no man is fully prepared for—or ever gets completely accustomed to. It's always a game of "keeping the lid on" when most everything about you, as well as your own instincts, tells you that you're a raving loon. Sometimes you are. But the climber who paws over the lip of a big wall, still whole in body and soul, has memories that no other sport can hope to match.

Mountaineering, in its extreme form, is the riskiest of all the climbing games. Sudden storms, avalanches that sweep entire mountains, horrific rock fall, physiological disorders from altitude and cold, are all out of a climber's hands and have drawn the curtain on hundreds of veterans. The old method of sieging the mountain, using armies of climbers, oxygen, and countless other helpful strategies, has slowly given way to "alpine" ascents, where a handful of climbers go for broke with little or no backup, are irreversibly committed, and survive only through personal prowess, iron will, and the grace of God. Successful parties invariably return with tales fantastic and astounding; and the ill-fated, by no count the minority, have stories none the less remarkable, though often with a tragic twist.

There are a hundred different games that fall somewhere in the middle, somewhere between the ace poised on a boulder in the British Virgin Islands, and the ironman who has just soloed Mt. Everest. Some make a specialty of ice climbing, clawing up overhanging icicles, or up gleaming arctic gullies. There are peak baggers who rarely use a rope, sport climbers who never use a rope, sea cliff climbers, limestone climbers, snow climbers, ski mountaineers, and people who own thousands of dollars of gear and only talk a good game. Chances are that the modern climber, whatever his specialty, has mastered the fundamentals while sport climbing. It remains the basic form in acquiring the knowledge of rope management, physical movement, and the mental conditioning requisite and applicable to any mode of ascent. The competent sport climber can readily cross over into big walls or big mountains and is qualified to make the transition quickly and safely. Happy climbing.

CHAPTER 9

Appendix: Sources

One of the happier consequences of a wider participation in rock climbing is easy access to good information. What follows is a listing of many of these sources.

Magazines, Books, and Videos

Climbing magazines are colorful and well-produced and, besides offering accounts of climbs and cliffs, are regularly a wealth of information on the latest gear and how it's used. Current guidebooks to just about every crag in America are published every few years and can be found in most local specialty mountain equipment shops. Climbing and mountaineering has perhaps the most active literary heritage of all sports, and many books and videos, from expedition accounts, to full color documentary pictorials are constantly being published.

Climbing Magazine
Post Office Box 339
Carbondale, CO 81623
(303) 963-9449

Chockstone Press, Inc.
Post Office Box 3505
Evergreen, CO 80439

The American Alpine Club
113 East 90th Street
New York, NY 10128
(212) 722-1628

Rock & Ice Magazine
Post Office Box 3595
Boulder, CO 80303
(303) 499-8410

The Mountaineers Books
306 Second Avenue W.
Seattle, WA 98119

Michael Chessler Books
Post Office Box 2436
Evergreen, CO 80439
(303) 670-0093

Guides and Instruction

There are many schools competent in the instruction and guiding of modern rock climbing. Most are members of the American Mountain Guides Association (reached at Post Office Box 4473, Bellingham WA 98227; 206-647-1167. In addition, many of the specialty outdoor shops have seasonal classes in rock climbing.

Equipment

Currrent issues of the climbing magazines are a good source of manufacturers and distributors of climbing gear. The magazines will also give indication of the diversity of equipment available; if your local outdoor shop only handles a few carabiners, nuts, and ropes, chances are good they are not knowledgeable about what is happening in the sport.

Rock Climbing Videos

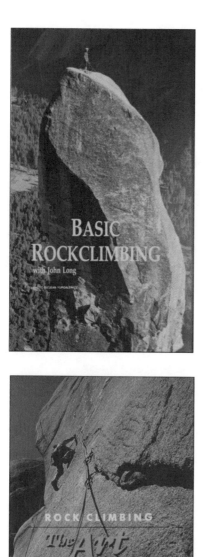

Video is a superb medium for the aspiring beginner to learn because it provides a look at the excellent technique of master climbers while a knowledgable observer explains the sublteties of their movements. John Long narrates and demonstrates technique in two such videos.

Basic Rock Climbing provides an introduction to the sport, filmed on location in Yosemite National Park. A fast pace runs through the fundamentals of climbing, from setting belays to basic climbing technique. The tape is ideal for one who knows nothing of climbing and wants an entertaining view of what is involved.

The Art of Leading takes a slightly more relaxed pace and deals with the unique problems encountered by leaders. Rope-work, setting belays, and strategies for successful ascents are addressed. Climbing techniques are expanded upon over the basic tape, with superb footage of aces Ron Kauk and Mari Gingery climbing difficult routes in dazzling fashion. Shot in Joshua Tree National Monument, one of the major U.S. areas, and Canyonlands National Park.

Each tape sells for $39.95 and is available from better outdoor stores or by sending a check or money order for $39.95 plus $2.00 shipping (total: $41.95) to:

CHOCKSTONE PRESS, INC.
Post Office Box 3505,
Evergreen, CO 80439.
Please specify which tape you want.

Glossary

The following is a compilation of some of the technical terms and jargon used throughout this book. This is a strictly American glossary; Brits, or the French, or Japanese undoubtedly use somewhat different terminology.

Aid: using means other than the action of hands, feet, and body English to get up a climb.

Anchor: a means by which climbers are infalibly secured to a cliff..

Armbar, Armlock: a means of holding onto a crack.

Belay: procedure of securing a climber by the use of the rope.

Biners: see Carabiners.

Bolt: an artificial anchor placed in a hole drilled for that purpose.

Bucket: a handhold, large enough to fully latch on to, like the lip of a bucket.

Cam: to lodge in a crack by counterpressure; that which lodges.

Carabiners: aluminum alloy rings equipped with a spring-loaded snap gate.

Ceiling: an overhang of sufficient size to loom overhead.

Chockstone: a rock lodged in a crack; now often also referring to nuts.

Clean: a description of routes that may be variously free of vegetation, loose rock, or even the need to place pitons. Also the act of removing nuts from a pitch.

Crux: the most difficult section of a climb or pitch.

Dihedral: an inside corner.

Drag: usually used in reference to the resistance of rope through carabiners.

Dynamic: lunge move.

Exposure: that relative situation where a climb has particularly noticeable sheerness.

Free: to climb using hands and feet only; the rope is only used to safeguard against injury, not for upward progress.

Gobis: hand abrasions.

Hangdog: where a leader lowers down from a piece of protection, then attempts the moves again without first pulling the rope through the protection and releading the pitch.

Jugs: like a jughandle.

Lead: to be first on a climb, placing protection with which to protect oneself.

Lieback: the climbing maneuver that entails pulling with the hands while pushing with the feet.

Line: the path of weakness which is the route.

Mantle: the climbing maneuver used to gain a single feature above one's head.

Move: movement; one of a series of motions necessary to gain climbing distance.

Nut: a mechanical device that, by various means, provides secure anchor to the cliff.

On sight: to climb a route without prior knowledge or experience of the moves.

Opposition: nuts, anchors, or climbing maneuvers that are held in place by the simultaneous stress of two forces working against each other.

Pinkpoint: to lead without falling a climb preprotected with anchors rigged with carabiners.

Pins: pitons.

Pitch: the section of rock between belays.

Pitons: metal spikes of various shapes used to provide anchor in cracks.

Placement: the quality of a nut or anchor.

Protection: the anchors used to safeguard the leader.

Prusik: both the knot and any means by which one mechanically ascends a rope.

Quickdraws: short slings with carabiners that help provide drag-free rope management for the leader.

Rappel: to descend a rope by means of mechanical brake devices.

Redpoint: to lead a route without falling or resting on pro.

Runout: the distance between two points of protection.

Second: the second one on a rope team, usually also the leader's belayer.

Sling: runner; a webbing loop used for a variety of purposes to anchor to the rock.

Smear: an ooze-like motion of the foot that uses the friction of the breadth of the sole to adhere to the rock.

Stance: a standing rest spot, often the site of the belay.

Stem: to bridge between two widely spaced holds.

Thin: a climb or hold of relatively featureless character.

Traverse: to move sideways, without altitude gain.